Beginner's Guide to
Crewel
Embroidery

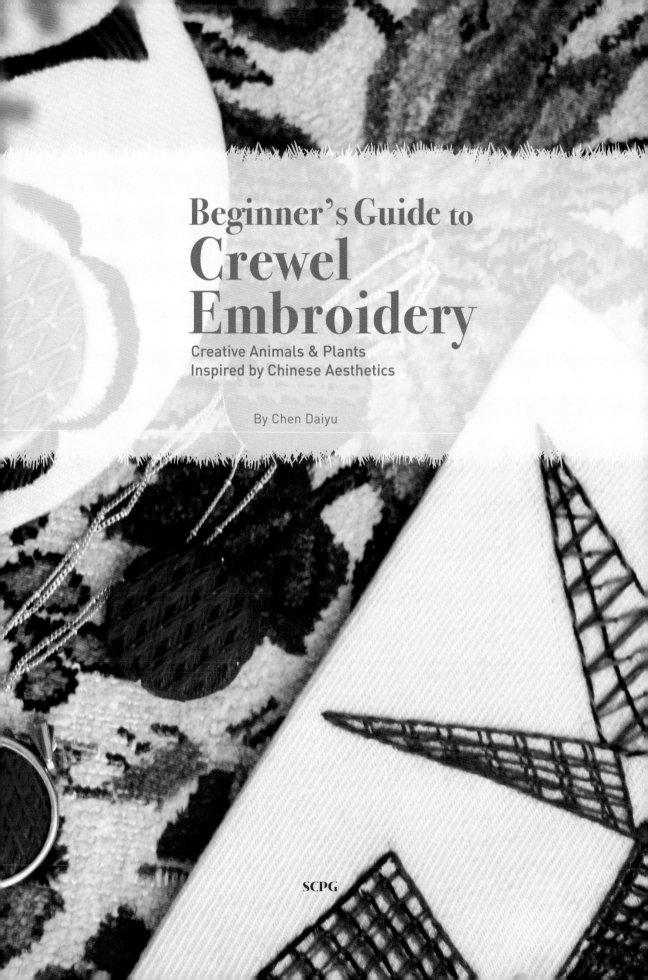

Beginner's Guide to
Crewel
Embroidery

Creative Animals & Plants
Inspired by Chinese Aesthetics

By Chen Daiyu

SCPG

Fig. 3 *Ginger Yellow Dream* (detail)
I have used crewel embroidery to capture my fantastical dream. In a sea of ginger yellow, various bizarrely shaped marine creatures abound, creating a surreal scene.

Text and Photographs: Chen Daiyu

Translation: Shelly Bryant

Cover Design: Shi Hanling

Interior Design: Hu Bin, Li Jing (Yuan Yinchang Design Studio)

Assistant Editor: Qiu Yan

Editor: Cao Yue

ISBN: 978-1-63288-029-1

Address any comments about *Beginner's Guide to Crewel Embroidery* to:

SCPG
401 Broadway, Ste. 1000
New York, NY 10013
USA

or

Shanghai Press and Publishing Development Co., Ltd.
Floor 5, No. 390 Fuzhou Road, Shanghai, China (200001)
Email: sppd@sppdbook.com

Printed in China by Shanghai Donnelley Printing Co., Ltd.

1   3   5   7   9   10   8   6   4   2

On page 1
Fig. 1 *Snake and Toad*
In traditional Chinese culture, the snake and the toad are considered two of the Five Poisons (the others being the scorpion, the centipede, and the gecko). However, in this context, "poison" does not refer to toxic substances. In folk customs, patterns depicting these five creatures are often posted in homes or embroidered on clothing to ward off evil spirits, prevent illness, and pray for peace and safety.

On pages 2–3
Fig. 2 *Crewel Necklaces*
Crewel necklaces feature geometric patterns are stitched with bright red wool embroidery thread, adding a simple yet striking accent to the overall outfit.

Bottom
Fig. 4 *Blue Squirrel*
Detail of *Wilderness Charm* on the facing page.

CONTENTS

Above
Fig. 5 *Wilderness Charm*
Amidst the layered, overlapping rocks, a towering giant tree grows, bearing a huge, mysterious fruit. A squirrel and a fawn seem to be drawn to this peculiar plant. The work carries a romantic, montage-like color palette.

To my mother,
with all my love and
gratitude.

FOREWORD

For me, wool embroidery is very special because it was the first type of embroidery I encountered when I formally entered the field. Going back to 2015, when I began systematically studying embroidery at the Royal School of Needlework (RSN) in London, UK, wool embroidery was the first type of

Fig. 7   Blue purple small peacock: (left) color draft, (right) stitch plan.

On facing page
Fig. 6 *Peacock*
This piece depicts a peacock perched on an imaginative vine, with a butterfly fluttering around. Peacocks and butterflies both symbolize wealth and auspiciousness in Chinese culture. This was my first crewel embroidery artwork.

embroidery introduced in the basic entry level courses. I remember on the first day I went to register at RSN, after the teacher gave a brief introduction to the school, she picked a few books from the library and asked me to read some classic cases. Then, she handed me paper and a pen, and instructed me to draw an A4-sized sketch within an hour. The sketch had to include an animal, some flowers, and some plants, and based on this, I was to choose two main color schemes and one auxiliary color scheme for the embroidery thread. At that time, I was a bit confused. Although I had graduated from an art college and systematically studied painting, and had also taught myself some basic stitching techniques, facing a type of embroidery I had never encountered before made it quite challenging for me to hand draw a sketch of this unfamiliar embroidery style. I took a deep breath, and after browsing through some teaching materials, I gradually developed a concept. I drew a vine plant that does not exist in reality and a small peacock in blue and purple hues. The teacher made some modifications to my sketch, and then, over the next seven days, I spent nearly 60 hours in class completing this piece.

Returning to the present, nearly ten years have passed since I embroidered my first wool embroidery piece. When I first started writing this book, I had a question: as a Chinese native, what does wool embroidery really mean to me, since Chinese embroidery is primarily done with silk thread, which is very fine, whereas the wool embroidery that originated in England uses thread that is more than ten times thicker than silk thread? This fundamental variation means that the visuals and the temperaments presented by wool embroidery and silk thread embroidery are distinctly different. It was for this reason that I decided to write a tutorial book from the perspective of a Chinese embroiderer, focusing on wool embroidery but with different subject matter from that found in traditional Western wool embroidery. After discussing with the editor, we chose the *Book of Songs*, a classic Chinese literary work (the oldest collection of poems in China, dating back three thousand years), as the entry point. From it, we selected some interesting plants and animals as the embroidery

Fig. 8 *Leisurely Afternoon*
Capturing a leisurely afternoon with crewel embroidery, sitting by the window, gazing at the lush greenery outside, enjoying a colorful array of tea and snacks in a tranquil atmosphere.

themes for this book. Traditional Western wool embroidery mainly uses geometric patterns to depict animals and plants. The animals and plants from the *Book of Songs* selected as themes for this book align well with the temperament of wool embroidery. At the same time, some of the plants in the book are unique to China, and some of the animals have not appeared in traditional wool embroidery works before, which gives the works in this book a unique flavor. Hopefully, this sense of both familiarity and novelty will provide readers with enjoyment and a fresh experience.

Additionally, I would like to share the artistic conception of traditional Chinese painting with everyone in this book. For example, *A Bite of Sweet Plant* (refer to page 53) is actually a wool embroidery piece that is very simple in both composition and stitching technique. From its composition, one can see the influence of traditional Chinese freehand painting. With just a few strokes, it does not seek to precisely replicate forms, but sketches out a clean, simple charm. By drawing inspiration from the simple compositions of traditional Chinese freehand painting and combining them with basic wool embroidery techniques, we can also create a distinctive wool embroidery piece.

During the process of writing this book, besides the design and embroidery, what made a particularly deep impression on me was the interaction with the editors while refining the manuscript. One of the aims of this book is to enable beginners to learn wool embroidery. As an artisan who has become accustomed to or has mastered embroidery techniques, I often don't realize that there is an invisible wall between those like me and readers who have never held the needle and thread. When people become accustomed to certain things, they unconsciously simplify their language expressions and may even overlook basic content and details. Such simplification and oversight hide a presumptive mindset in the speaker. Often the steps that authors think are unnecessary are actually crucial for readers. I want to express my sincere gratitude to my editors for the questions they raised during the proofreading process. It is these questions that allowed this book to be perfected.

It is this shift in perspective that made the process of writing the manuscript more relaxed and enjoyable for me. I found that my perspective changed throughout the process of embroidery, writing, and proofreading, bringing this complex process from the perspective of an author skilled in embroidery techniques to that of a reader with no experience in embroidery. I began to think and answer every question from the reader's perspective, taking the time to carefully describe and photograph each step.

I hope this book can serve as a bridge for beginners to advance towards higher level techniques.

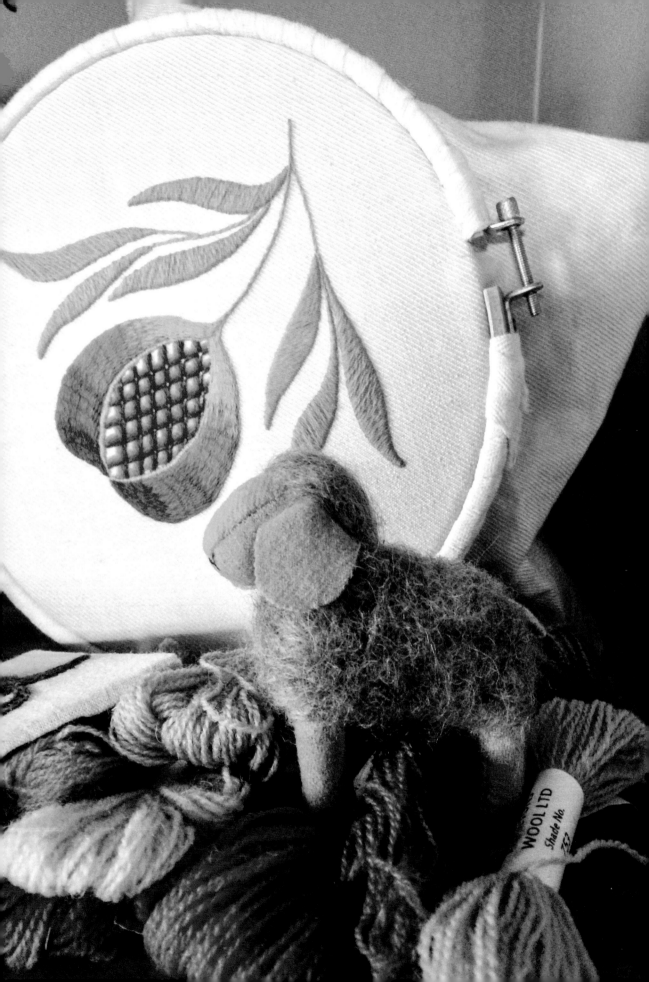

CHAPTER ONE
Materials, Tools, and Preparation

This book aims to give readers a taste of the joy of crewel embroidery done with the simplest tools. This chapter will introduce you to the embroidery threads, needles, fabrics for crewel embroidery, and steps for stretching, preparing you to create the works featured in later chapters.

Wool Thread

The crewel embroidery thread I frequently use is produced in the UK by Appleton. Appleton's range includes a rich variety of wool thread with over four hundred colors, which come in both skeins (bundles of thread each 8 meters long) and hanks (longer coils of thread, measuring 160 meters). Generally, for household or small projects, using skeins is sufficient.

It is worth noting that wool thread is dyed in batches, and there is no guarantee that colors will be exactly consistent across different batches. Before starting to create an embroidery piece, it is advisable to estimate the usage of each color thread fairly accurately to prevent running out of thread and needing to add more later, which might result in uneven colors on the embroidered surface.

To use a skein of embroidery thread, keep the paper waistband on the thread in order to keep the thread from unraveling. Then, find that correct end of the thread.

Fig. 10 The thread end is generally located on the outer edge of the thread bundle.

On facing page
Fig. 9 *Peach*
In Chinese mythology, peaches are celestial fruits grown in heaven, symbolizing longevity. I have used delicate gradient shades of pink to depict the tender, fresh quality of peaches, with grid patterns highlighting the fullness of the fruit's flesh.

If pulling the thread end causes tension in the remaining part, causing it to bundle up, it is wrong end or the "thread tail." Be careful not to pull the thread tail. The correct thread end is the one that can be easily pulled (usually on the outer part of the entire skein).

After finding the thread end, pull out a segment of thread about half a meter long, approximately the length from the wrist to the shoulder, and then cut it with small scissors. Generally, this is the length used each time. Using thread that is too short may require rethreading of the needle and involve unnecessary starting steps. Thread that is too long can easily wear out the thread, causing it to flatten or even break.

Embroidery Needle

The main types of needles for crewel embroidery are chenille needles and tapestry needles, with the recommended brand being John James. These are usually available in single-size packs of 6 and 25 needles.

The main difference between chenille and tapestry needles is that the former has a sharp tip, typically used for stitches that go through the fabric, while the latter has a blunt tip, primarily used for stitches above the fabric that involve wrapping, such as whipped wheel stitch. The embroidery needles used in this book default to chenille size 22 needles and tapestry size 22 needles.

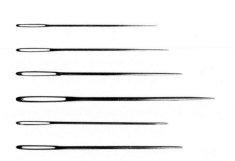

Fig. 11 From top to bottom: chenille size 24, 22, 20, 18 needles, tapestry size 24, 22 needles.

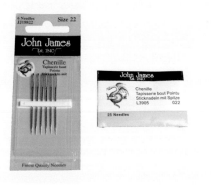

Fig. 12 John James embroidery needles: single size pack of 6 (left) and single size pack of 25 (right).

Fabric

In general, there is a wide range of fabrics that can be used for crewel embroidery. Any fabric with medium thickness, no elasticity, and a non-smooth surface can be used. Cotton and linen cloth with medium thickness, cotton canvas, twill cotton fabric, and short pile fabrics used in autumn and winter seasons are all suitable fabric options.

Fig. 13 From left to right: plant-dyed linen, cotton and linen cloth, washed cotton fabric, professional wool embroidery twill fabric.

Basic Steps for Stretching

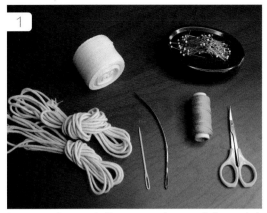

Basic stretching tools (from top to bottom, left to right): 4-cm wide herringbone cotton tape, magnetic pin cushion with bead pins, cotton piping cords, threading needles, hand-sewn polyester thread, and curved-tip scissors.

Fold the wide edge of the embroidery fabric inward by one centimeter, then fold it in half and find the center point, marking it with a pencil or water soluble pen.

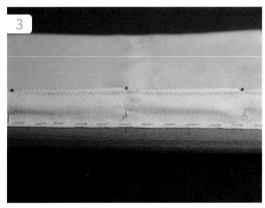

Align the marked center point on the embroidery fabric with the center point of the herringbone cotton tape on one side of the embroidery frame and secure it with bead pins. Secure the center point, then roughly secure the two ends of the embroidery fabric.

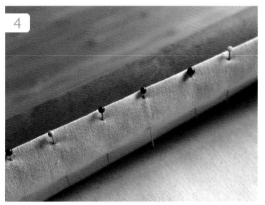

After securing both ends, gradually add bead pins at intervals, with each pin spaced approximately 1.5 cm apart.

The picture shows the back of the herringbone tape after all bead pins have been secured.

Thread a chenille size 22 needle with polyester thread and start sewing around from the center point secured by bead pins toward the left side.

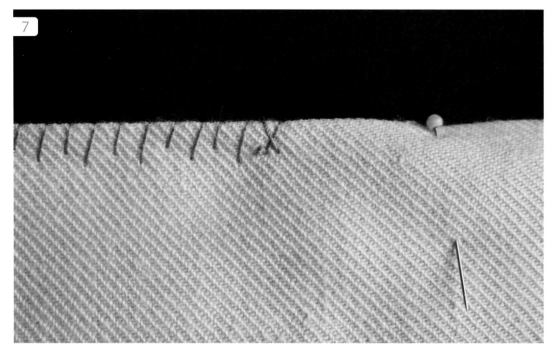

Attention should be paid to ensuring that the lengths of each stitch are not the same. If all stitches are at the same latitude, there is a risk that when tightening the thread at the end, the herringbone cotton tape on the embroidery frame may be pulled due to the force points being on the same horizontal line. Complete the stitching on the left side first, then proceed to the stitching on the right side, and complete the stitching on the other end of the embroidery frame in the same manner.

When reaching the end, finish with backstitch.

Insert the vertical strip (the wood strip with holes) into both sides of the horizontal strip (without holes) and secure it with a cotter pin. It is important to note that the holes on the vertical strips on both sides of the embroidery frame should be symmetrically placed.

The embroidery frame should be laid flat on the embroidery stand.

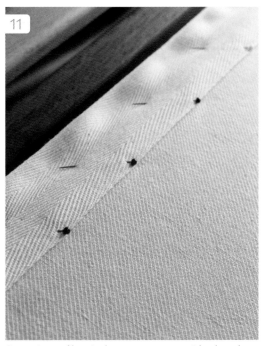

Cut a piece of herringbone cotton tape with a length equal to the unfixed edge of the embroidery fabric, as shown in the picture, and secure it with bead pins. This step is for the final stretch and fixing of the embroidery fabric.

As shown in the picture, insert the needle from the right side of the herringbone cotton tape and exit from the left side.

Make another stitch in the same position.

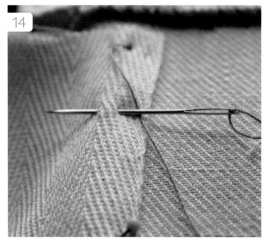

When moving to the next stitch, you can remove the bead pins used to temporarily fix the fabric.

Continue stitching at approximately 1.5 cm intervals.

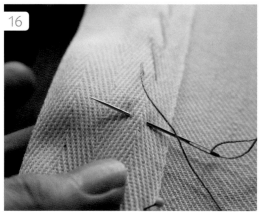

As shown in the picture, when stitching, you can use your thumb and index finger for assistance. The index finger slightly lifts the fabric from the back, making it easier for the needle to pierce through.

Pay attention to pull each stitch tight, creating a slightly raised strip where the herringbone tape and the embroidery fabric meet. This is beneficial for later stretching at both ends.

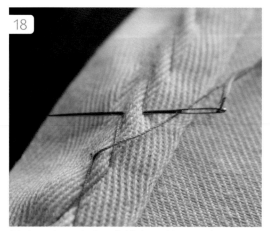

Stitch to the end, then finish by making 4 to 5 backstitches.

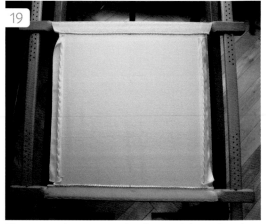

The picture shows an overhead view of the embroidery frame after being stitched and fixed both vertically and horizontally.

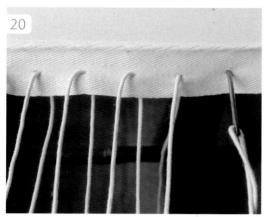

Thread an iron curved needle with cotton cords and stitch from left to right with approximately 3 cm spacing between stitches. Leave about 1 meter of cotton cord at the left end, which will later be used for wrapping.

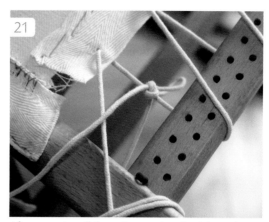

After wrapping all the cotton cord to the right end, return to the starting point on the left and secure the cord end with a knot, as shown in the picture.

After securing the left side, moving from left to right, manually tighten each stitch to near the limit, and then secure the cord end on the right side in the same way.

The excess cord can be wrapped as shown in the picture. There is no need to cut it. This way, the same piece of cotton cord can be reused for framing different sized works.

The picture shows the result after completing the stretching. At this point, the fabric is in a completely wrinkle free and tight state, and you can hear a drum-like sound when you flick it with your fingers. If the fabric appears soft, first loosen the cotton cords at both ends, adjust the position of the cotter pins, and then tighten the cotton cords.

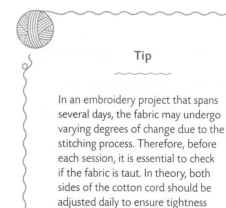

Tip

In an embroidery project that spans several days, the fabric may undergo varying degrees of change due to the stitching process. Therefore, before each session, it is essential to check if the fabric is taut. In theory, both sides of the cotton cord should be adjusted daily to ensure tightness before beginning to embroider.

CHAPTER TWO
Glittering Golden Pond

I n the earliest Chinese poetry collection, the *Book of Songs*, one of the
most widely circulated poems is "Guān Jū" (关雎). The poem mentions
"floating hearts" (荇菜, xìngcài), a waterborne herb with small yellow
flowers. Based on the color of its leaves, it can be classified into various types
such as white floating heart, red floating heart, purple floating heart, and
multicolored floating heart. This colorful vegetable can also be cooked into
soups. Students traditionally drink a bowl of this soup before taking exams,
symbolizing the pursuit of great achievements in their studies.

In Chinese culture, the carp symbolizes good fortune. One of China's

On facing page
Fig. 14 Woolen Coat with Floral Pattern
Embroidering a branch of flowers and leaves in a Morandi color palette on the collar of a woolen coat
adds a fresh and unique touch.

most famous poet Li Bai (701–762) wrote a poem about it: *The three-foot carp in the Yellow River originally resides in Mengjin. Unable to transform into a dragon, it returns home to accompany ordinary fish.* The poem contains the ancient Chinese myth of Carp Leaping over the Dragon Gate. According to the legend, if a carp can jump over the Dragon Gate, it will transform into a dragon, symbolizing success in one's career and elevation in status.

As the first project in this book, I have chosen a pair of carps and multicolored floating hearts as the theme, combining the auspicious symbolism of both to depict a scene of harmony.

Preparatory Work

1

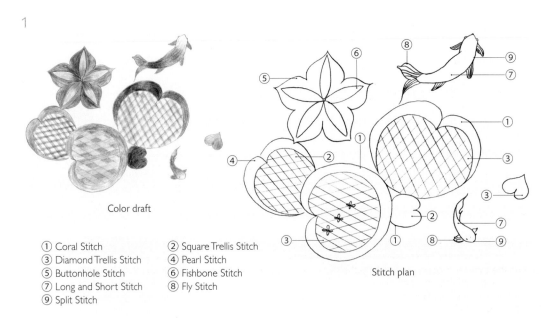

Color draft

Stitch plan

① Coral Stitch
② Square Trellis Stitch
③ Diamond Trellis Stitch
④ Pearl Stitch
⑤ Buttonhole Stitch
⑥ Fishbone Stitch
⑦ Long and Short Stitch
⑧ Fly Stitch
⑨ Split Stitch

First, prepare the stitch plan and color draft for reference.

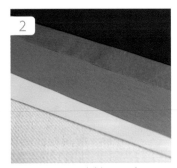

Prepare water soluble transfer paper. Please note that there is a type of transfer paper with non-water soluble ink. If using this type of transfer paper, ensure that the embroidery completely covers the traced lines.

On the outline draft, trace or make another copy using transparent tracing paper (or photocopy) for use in pattern transfer.

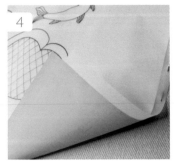

Take a piece of transfer paper and place it between the fabric and the outline draft paper.

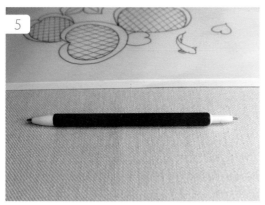

Prepare a drawing pen. Alternatively, you can use a ballpoint pen with no ink.

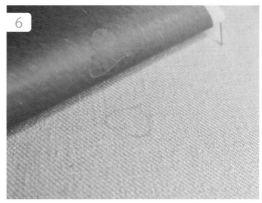

The yellow transfer paper in the photo may not appear clear on the fabric, but it is usable in actual operation. To make it clearer for readers, it has been changed to green transfer paper here.

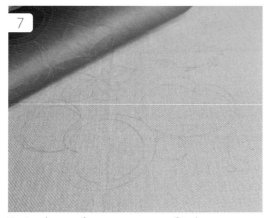

During the transfer process, you can flip the paper up to check if the traced lines are clear at any time. However, ensure that when checking, your hand stabilizes the two layers of paper on top to prevent any offset in position when continuing the drawing.

The result after completing the transfer.

Choose your embroidery thread according to the color draft. During the embroidery process, colors can be added as needed based on actual requirements.

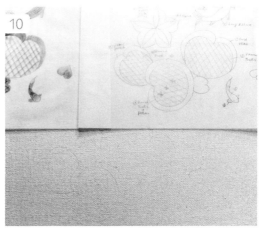

Before starting the embroidery, double check the color draft and the stitch plan.

Stitching Steps

This chapter is an introductory project that will guide you through the embroidery process, introducing the nine fundamental stitch techniques of crewel embroidery. With the trellis stitch as the central technique and complemented by stitches like fishbone stitch, long and short stitch, fly stitch, and others, the entire piece utilizes 12 colors and takes approximately 12 hours to complete. It is hoped that readers can gain a basic understanding of crewel embroidery through this study.

Floating Heart

🧶 Three Stitch Cast On

Firstly, as the foundation for starting stitches, it is essential to master the three stitch cast on technique. Unless otherwise specified, it will be referred to as the three stitch technique in the following text.

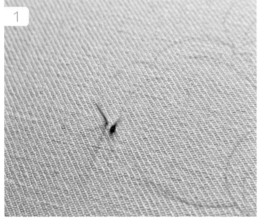

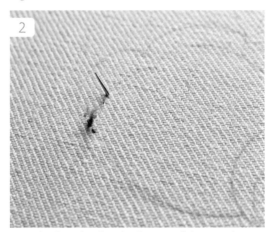

Casting on, insert the needle from the front, leaving the thread end on the fabric surface.

Near the thread end, make three small short stitches individually.

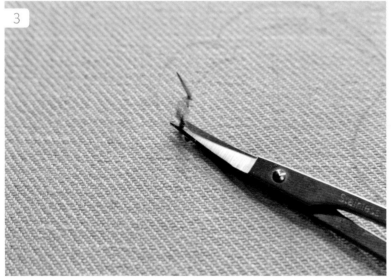

Trim the thread end close to the fabric from the front, then gently pull the embroidery thread to test its firmness. This completes the entire cast on process. Similarly, when a section of the embroidery is completed, the three stitch technique can be used to secure the end. The only difference is that there will not be a thread end generated during the finishing. Instead, the embroidery thread is cut directly on the fabric after the three stitches are made.

🧶 Square Trellis Stitch

Trellis is a common basic stitch in crewel embroidery, typically used to fill large areas, such as leaves or the bodies of large animals. It is an interesting stitch that can be combined with multiple colors to create various layers.

In this section, we will use four embroidery threads: number 696, 697, 606, 464 and a chenille size 22 needle.

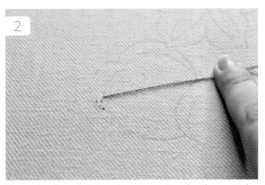

First, take thread 696 and cast on using the three stitch technique. Then, start stitching from the inner contour of the floating heart leaf, pulling the thread with the right hand, forming a horizontal angle of around 15 degrees, while using the left-hand finger to assist in fixing the embroidery thread.

With the right hand holding the needle, insert the needle at the position shown in the picture. The needle passes through the middle of the thread because it helps to keep the thread parallel without shifting.

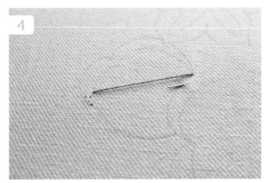

Come out from the back. Take care not to allow the needle to fully emerge, instead, use the tip of needle to check if the distance from the first stitch is appropriate before completing the stitch. The distance is approximately 6 mm.

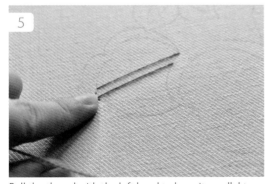

Pull the thread with the left hand to keep it parallel to the first thread, then insert the needle to secure it.

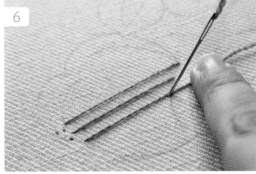

This image shows the details of inserting the needle. As in step 3, the needle passes through the middle of the thread.

Repeat the above steps to continue stitching.

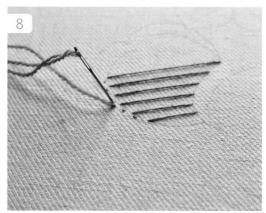

After completing the lower part, exit the needle from the side and finish with the three stitch technique. After finishing with three stitches, make a few more stitches and move to the upper part of the embroidery. Take care to use small stitches here to avoid directly pulling a long stitch on the back, which may interfere with later stitches.

Using small stitches, gradually progress to the upper part and continue completing the remaining section. Please note that, for the entire pattern to remain parallel and consistent spacing, do not start a new cast on directly from the upper side of the pattern.

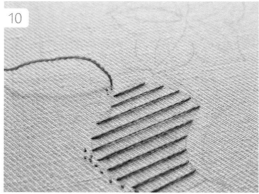

Complete the remaining stitches in the same manner as the lower part, then finish with the three stitch technique.

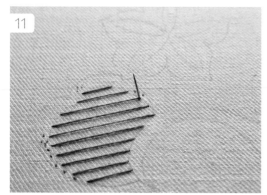

Start with the three stitch technique. As shown in the picture, the first stitch emerges at the end of one of the horizontal lines.

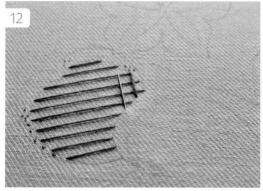

The first vertical stitch is crucial because the remaining stitches will be based on it as a standard.

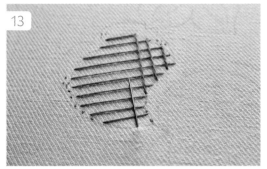

Continue with the vertical stitch, using the needle as a ruler to measure and stitch at the same time.

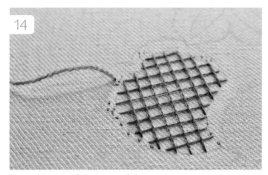

Complete the first layer of the grid pattern.

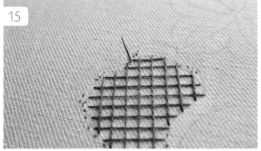

Switch to thread 697 and cast on at the indicated position in the picture.

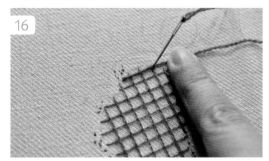

The stitches of the second layer should be very close to the first layer but not overlapping. Start with the horizontal stitches here.

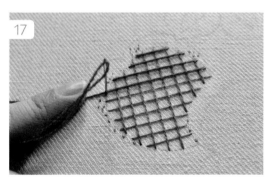

Take your time as you stitch, always maintaining parallel lines.

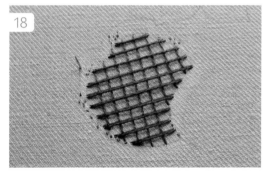

The completed effect of the second layer of horizontal stitches.

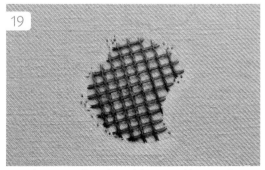

Complete vertical stitches of the second layer in the same manner.

For the third layer, use purple thread, number 606.

The result after completing the embroidery with the purple thread.

Next, move on to the final step, which I like to call it "nailing sesame." Use thread 464 here.

As shown in the picture, stitch diagonally upward from the bottom. The exit point is on the topmost purple layer, located at the top left corner of the first intersection in the top row. The exit angle is a 45-degree slant.

The entry point is at the opposite bottom right corner of the intersection, also at a 45-degree slant. The purpose of the blue thread is to anchor each intersecting point of the topmost purple thread. For beginners, it may get caught on the thread below, which is fine, as long as the purple intersection points are secured.

The finished effect of "nailing sesame" is shown in the image.

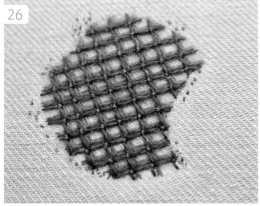

Anchor all the intersections in order from left to right and top to bottom.

Diamond Trellis Stitch

The next step is to finish the second floating heart leaf. We will use a derivative stitch of square trellis stitch called diamond trellis stitch. The main difference is that the angles of the horizontal and vertical stitches are obtuse instead of perpendicular.

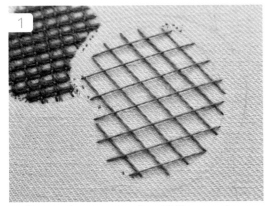

As shown in the image, use thread 567 to complete the first layer of stitches, paying attention to the angles where the horizontal and vertical lines intersect.

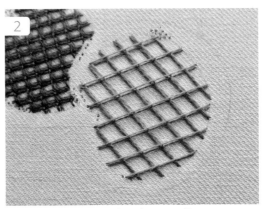

Use thread 463 to complete the second layer.

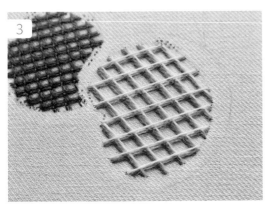

Use thread 551 to overlay the third layer.

Overlay the fourth layer with thread 462. The picture shows the result after completing the four layers of stitches.

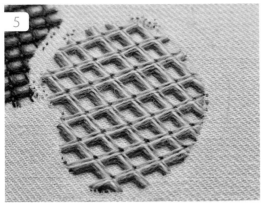

Use thread 697 to anchor the intersections.

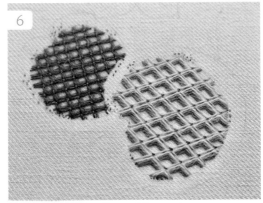

Comparison of the effects of the two leaves.

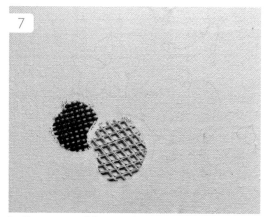

Bird's eye view of the completed embroidered section.

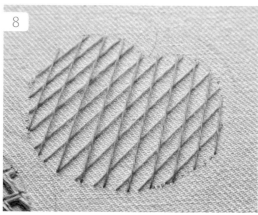

For the third leaf, continue using the diamond trellis stitch with a slight variation. This time, the angle between the horizontal and vertical lines is acute. Embroider the first layer with thread 695.

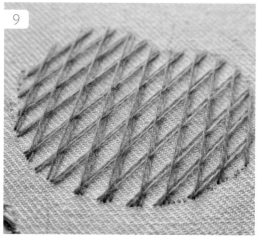

For the second layer, use the contrasting blue thread, number 463.

For the final layer, use the dark grape purple thread, number 606.

Anchor the intersections of the third layer of purple thread. Use a red purple thread, number 149, close in color to the dark grape purple, to make the sesame-like stitches blend into the third layer.

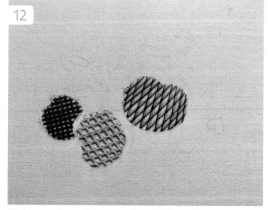

Bird's eye view of the completed effect of the three leaves.

🧶 Pearl Stitch

The pearl stitch is a unique stitch in crewel embroidery that combines both piercing through the fabric and wrapping the thread above the surface. In this stitch, double threads are used to achieve a fuller three-dimensional effect. Note: Double threads here mean passing two threads through one needle, then tying a knot at one end. It is not folding and knotting a single thread after passing it through the needle hole.

First, look at the detailed image to gain a rough understanding of this stitching technique.

Using thread 567, start with three stitch technique in the bottom right corner of the first leaf. Then make a diagonal stitch (with a stitch length of about 5 mm), immediately followed by pulling the needle out at the lower left corner of the diagonal stitch.

As shown in the picture, wrap around the first diagonal stitch, pass the thread through the stitch and then tighten it.

After tightening, it will form a small bead-like structure.

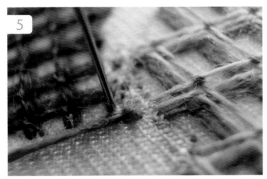

Next, make another diagonal stitch towards the upper left corner, similar to the first stitch, with a vertical short stitch of about 5 mm.

Similarly, after completing the short stitch, exit at its lower left corner, wrap around the short stitch, pass it underneath the short stitch, and then tighten the stitch.

Zooming out, we can see the entry angle of the stitch and the size comparison between the pearl stitch and the entire embroidered surface.

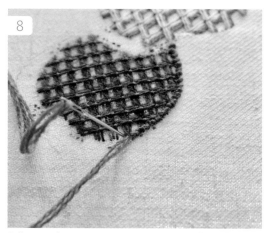

Following the same manner, continue stitching along the edge of the leaf to complete the remaining part.

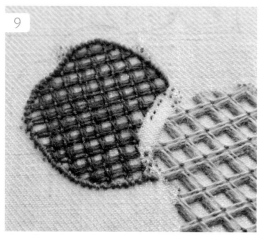

The effect of completing the first round of pearl stitch.

Next, embroider the second round of pearl stitch.

In the second round of embroidery, the thread changes to number 606, and returns to a single strand to create variation from the first round.

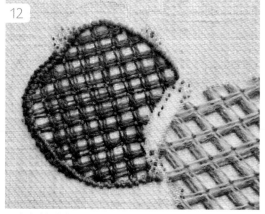

Only half of the second round needs to be completed, but in actual embroidery, the color of thread can vary according to personal preference. I chose to embroider half a circle because I wanted to present a touch of dark purple in this section.

Continue with the third round, using lighter purple thread, number 604.

In the process of embroidery, you will gradually discover that the 5-mm short vertical stitch in the upper left corner may vary slightly depending on the specific shape of the pattern. Sometimes, this vertical stitch may appear almost like a horizontal one. With greater proficiency, you will make it as short as 3 mm, or even 1 mm, before proceeding with the wrapping. Of course, all variations should be based on specific needs.

During the embroidery process, if the threads catch during wrapping, you can switch to a tapestry needle, preferably size 22. However, note that this needle has a blunt tip, making it less sharp when piercing the fabric. You can choose between the chenille needle and the tapestry needle based on your preferences and needs.

For the next round, we will switch to the brown red thread, number 125.

Embroider slowly next to the previous round, trying not to leave blank spaces between the two circles.

The result after completing one dark circle and one light circle.

For the final round, we will return to the purple thread, number 102.

Moving from blue to purple, from purple to red, and then back to purple, the pearl stitches are completed.

The effect of a single leaf when viewed from above.

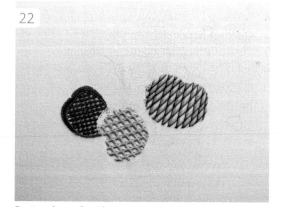

During the embroidery process, it is important to periodically review the work. After completing a section, you can stand the embroidery frame up and stand about a meter away to examine the piece to see if any adjustments are needed. Then proceed with the next step of embroidery.

🧶 Coral Stitch

The coral stitch is a primarily knotted technique that can be done with either a single thread or double threads. It is recommended for beginners to initially practice with double threads, as this results in stronger knots and a better overall effect.

For the first round, use double thread 567 for embroidery. At the position shown in the picture, start the stitching with three stitch technique, then pull the thread straight toward the left side.

As shown in the picture, use your left hand to secure a section of the thread and insert the needle approximately 5 mm from its upper end.

After inserting the needle, pull it to the back, then come out from the center of the circle formed on the front.

After coming out with the needle, tighten it to create a coral stitch with a trailing tail.

Continuing in the same manner, proceed to knot along the pattern as shown.

Take a different perspective to view the position of the needle as it comes out.

The appearance after completing the first round.

The result after completing five rounds with coral stitch. The embroidery threads used are three shades of blue (number 461, 463, 464), and number 551 goose yellow, for the arcs. I used three goose yellow arcs to complement the inner yellow section.

As mentioned earlier, after completing a section, it is important to review the overall effect.

For the last leaf, first look at the final effect. From the picture, it can be seen that there are a few strands of gradient colored thread interspersed within the single-colored threads.

The gradient effect is achieved by combining two threads of closely related color schemes (number 551 and 554).

Please note that while embroidering with double threads, you may encounter situations where the needle comes out from between the two threads. This is permissible.

To enhance the richness of the leaf surface, even though you are using the same stitching technique, you can use colors flexibly. In this section, you can incorporate some threads from the purple red color scheme. This helps to complement the colors of the surrounding leaves and the purple within this particular leaf.

Referring to step 13, you can flexibly mix the purple and yellow threads, embroidering 5 to 6 rounds. The image shows the partial effect after completion.

In this small leaf, there is a combination of purple, red, light yellow, goose yellow, and sky-blue colors.

The overall effect after completing all three leaves.

🪡 Buttonhole Stitch

The buttonhole stitch is a rather unique technique in which the front and back stitches remain interconnected. This means that the exit point of the back stitch secures the thread of the front stitch. The key to this stitching technique is to maintain consistent spacing between each stitch.

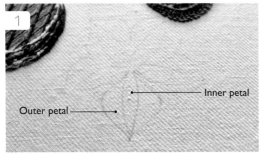

Begin embroidering the flower part. Since completing the entire embroidery may take a week or even longer, the ink markings from the water soluble pen may fade. Before continuing with the embroidery, it is advisable to retrace the parts that need to be embroidered using a water soluble pen. Divide each petal into two main parts, the central part, referred to as the inner petal, and the parts on both sides, referred to as the outer petal.

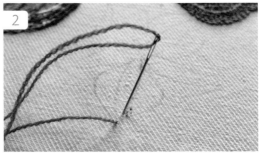

Using thread 904, start with three stitch technique, coming out at the tip of the petal. Then, make short stitches along the right tracing line of inner petal for approximately 5 mm.

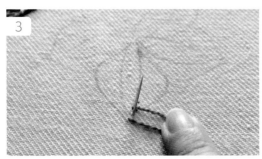

Bring the needle back out in the middle between the front and back stitches. Here, you can use the finger of your left hand to press down on the thread on the surface, allowing the thread to maintain its length before coming out.

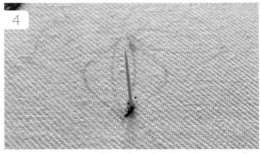

After coming out, pull the thread tight and position the needle above the first stitch.

Starting from the fourth stitch, insert the needle along the inner petal tracing line, then come out again in the middle between the two stitches. Note: The exit point here is on the outline of the outer petal, not on the inner petal.

Moving forward several stitches, as shown in the picture, each exit point is on the outer petal outline, while the entry points are on the inner petal outline.

The key to the buttonhole stitch is to keep each stitch close to the next, meaning that each exit and entry point should be as close together as possible for a neat appearance.

Additionally, each time you come out with the needle, pull the thread tight to maintain moderate tension in the thread from the previous stitch.

At the turning points, because the inner arc is shorter than the outer arc, the stitches on the inner petal should be close together, while the stitches on the outer petal can be spaced slightly apart. This is necessary for a perfect turn.

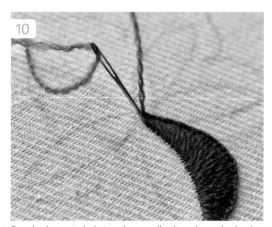

For the last stitch, bring the needle directly to the back and secure it with three stitch technique to finish.

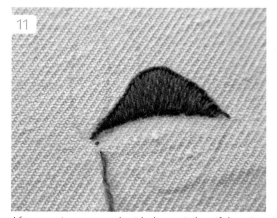

After securing your work with three stitches, if there is excess thread, continue embroidering the outer petal on the other side with it.

The image shows the appearance after completing one side of the outer petal. Repeat the same process for the remaining outer petals.

🪡 Fishbone Stitch

The fishbone stitch has a fishbone like appearance and is commonly used for embroidering leaves. It can be done in a single color or gradient colors. When changing colors, you can use two needles alternately. It is one of the common stitches in crewel embroidery.

Prepare a set of gradient wool threads, number 696, 695, 554, and 551.

Using thread 551 and starting with the three stitch technique, come out from the top, then take a stitch toward the center of the inner petal, about 5 mm.

Bring the needle back out to the left side near the top of the first stitch.

Then, insert the needle on the right side at the end of the first stitch.

Use the same method for the right-side stitches, meaning the needle comes out on the right side near the top of the first stitch, then insert the needle on the left side at the end of the first stitch. After that, bring the needle back to the left side.

Continue stitching in the same manner. For beginners, remember that accuracy is more important than speed for each exit and entry point. Pay special attention to avoiding leaving gaps between the stitches coming out and the brown outer petals.

After completing a few stitches, you can see the initial form. At this point, you can introduce the thread in next color, number 554. You can set aside the needle threaded with number 551 on the side of the embroidery surface without cutting it.

After starting with the three stitch technique using thread 554, come out directly from the point B, which is below the last stitch of thread 551 (point A). So be careful to leave a gap of about 2 mm for thread 554 to come out below the last stitch of 551.

Use thread 554 to make stitches on both sides following the stitching method from steps 2 to 5.

Then, set aside the needle with thread 554 in place, and use 551 to make another set of stitches (a set refers to one stitch on the left and one on the right, hereafter referred to as one set). Next, alternate between 554 and 551, which is taking one set of stitches with thread 554, followed by one set with 551.

After stitching two sets each with threads 551 and 554, finish 551 with the three stitch technique. Continue embroidering with 554 until reaching the position shown in the picture.

Using the same method of transition, after thread 554 has taken 3 to 4 sets, you can introduce thread 695.

13

Stitch one set with thread 695 until you reach the area near the flower's center. At this point, you can introduce the thread in last color, number 696.

14

A petal can be completed with three or four colors in a gradient, depending on the size of the petal and the desired effect. There is no strict rule. During regular practice, you can also try transitioning from dark threads to light threads to see the resulting effect.

15

The picture shows that the inner petal's darkest color, thread 904, is the same as the color of outer petal. If there is enough excess thread, you can use this section of thread to embroider the adjacent outer petal without starting a new thread.

16

In the embroidery sequence, you can follow the order of completing one outer petal and then one inner petal to cover the entire surface.

Alternatively, as shown in the picture, you can first complete all the outer petals and then move on to the inner petal sections.

Regardless of the sequence, the key is the current length of the thread in hand. After some experience, you will find that embroidery is not a rigid arrangement, but more about letting the thread follow your heart.

You can also make slight changes when embroidering each inner petal. For example, the first inner petal has more of threads 551 and 554, then you can emphasize 695 and 696 for the second inner petal. This way, the embroidered pattern becomes rich and dynamic, with no two petals being the same.

The top view of the completed flower.

Next, embroider the small leaf hidden beneath the large leaves.

First, use thread 551 to embroider the first layer of grid pattern using square trellis stitch.

Using the same technique, complete the second and third layers of grid pattern with threads 554 and 969. Finally, use thread 149 to anchor the intersections.

For the outer contour of the small leaf, use threads 149 and 606 from the purple color scheme. Complete it with coral stitch using single thread. Embroider 3 to 4 layers from the inside out, with a predominant color of purple red and adding some coffee color tones.

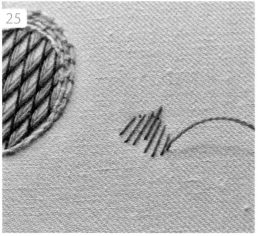

Be more casual with the final small leaf. Use thread 125 to make several vertical stitches first.

Then, add intersecting lines to create the diamond trellis stitch effect.

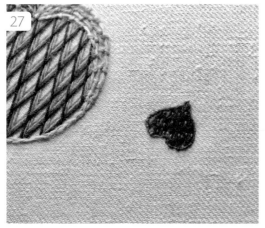

You can add more intersecting lines to make it denser. Finally, use thread 696 to anchor intersections in the interior and use the coral stitch to complete the outer contour.

At this point, the majority of the embroidery is completed.

Carp

Split Sitch, Long and Short Stitch, Fly Stitch

The split stitch is perfect for outlining. The long and short stitch is one of the most common stitches in crewel embroidery. It involves alternating between long and short stitches, and it is mainly used to depict gradient images. The fly stitch is commonly used to embroider leaves and bird feathers. It involves advancing vertically by taking one stitch and anchoring it with another.

The final part is the two carp fish, using threads 125, 149, 604, and 606. The stitching technique for the fish is mainly composed of two parts: long and short stitch for the fish body, and the fly stitch for the fish fins and tail.

Start with the large fish. Observe the embroidery surface to determine if it needs to be re-outlined.

Before starting the long and short stitch, it is useful to first learn the split stitch. Begin with thread 606, using the three stitch technique. Make a short stitch of about 3 mm, then insert the needle back through the middle of the previous stitch and come out.

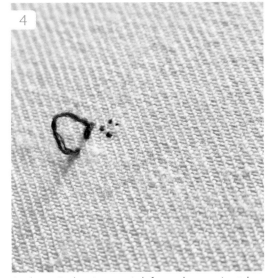

As shown in the picture, stitch forward, approximately 5 mm.

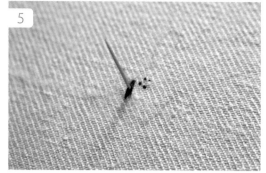

Similarly, go back to the middle of the previous stitch to come out. Continue this process to outline the entire outer contour of the fish body. The split stitch is a basic stitching technique. The key is to make each stitch fine and closely woven so that the outline embroidered is firm, not loose and floppy. Avoid using large stitches to save time.

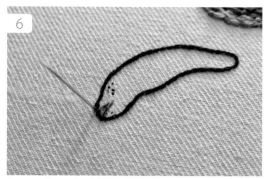

Starting from the fish head with thread 604, use the three stitch technique to make three stitches of varying lengths. When coming out, angle the needle diagonally along the outer edge of the outline.

Insert the needle from the outside inward at a 45-degree angle, maintaining varying lengths for the stitches.

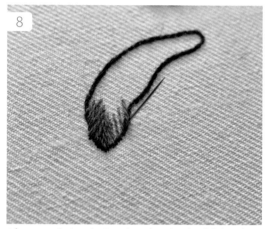

After completing the initial stitches for the fish head, gradually introduce thread 606.

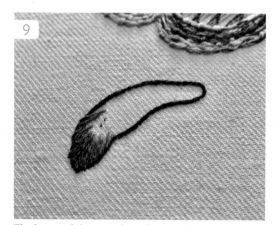

The long and short stitch is a basic stitching technique in crewel embroidery, though it is challenging due to the color blending involved. Patience is crucial when working with this stitch.

After a certain number of stitches, it is important to be skillful in positioning the needle when coming out. Coming out from the middle of the previous layer may occasionally split some threads. This is acceptable.

If there are noticeable gaps, slowly fill them in.

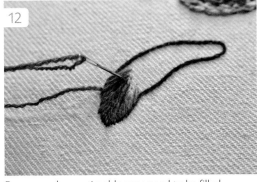

Even some less noticeable gaps need to be filled.

Continue embroidering from the outer contour toward the inside with thread 606.

Continue until half of the fish body is filled.

Start incorporating thread 125.

Similarly, start from the outer contour and embroider from the outside inward.

Construct the layer of thread 125 from right to left carefully.

Next, introduce the final thread, number 149.

Be patient and slowly incorporate thread 149 into the previous layer, maintaining the diagonal entry approach.

The picture shows the completed effect of color overlay. Note: In actual practice, if you find the transition from purple to red challenging, you can choose all four colors in the purple scheme. Skipping colors in the gradient overlay is an intermediate to advanced technique. Do not worry if the result is not ideal. You can practice it until you become more proficient.

Near the tail, gradually make the stitches smaller and fill the tail area slowly.

The completed effect of the entire fish body.

Next, use the fly stitch, taking one of the fish fins as an example. Start by coming out from the top, then take a short stitch vertically, about 3 mm.

Come out from the left side near the top of the first stitch.

25

Then, insert the needle on the right side.

26

Come back to the top of the first stitch (above the horizontal line formed in steps 24 to 25) and come out.

27

After coming out, pull the embroidery thread tight. Once the thread is taut, insert a vertical stitch in the middle of the horizontal line to secure it. In other words, insert the needle below the mid-point of the horizontal line to anchor it.

28

Proceed with the second set of stitches as shown in the picture. This involves coming out on the left, going in on the right, and then inserting a vertical stitch to secure the horizontal line formed by the first two stitches. This naturally creates a V-shaped stitch.

29

Ensure that each middle stitch is in a straight line.

30

As you approach the end, the right side of the thread is already close to the fish body. At this point, you can continue to complete the left side stitches without inserting additional stitches in the middle. In the remaining space on the left side, embroider parallel lines by coming out from the top and going in at the bottom, filling the entire fish fin.

Complete all the fish fins in the same manner.

Finally, complete the fish tail using the fly stitch, incorporating gradient colors.

To incorporate gradient colors, you can refer to the earlier steps of gradient stitching in fishbone stitch part. Here, threads of four colors are used from top to bottom as shown by the red arrow: number 696, 695, 554, and 758.

The completed effect of embroidering with three gradient threads.

To create a natural transition between the fish body and tail, reintroduce purple thread, number 149.

Transition between the fish body and tail is done with diagonal stitches. Start a few stitches with thread 149 in red purple and then add 697 in brown.

Finally, sequentially add yellow tones with threads 554 and 551.

The fish tail is completed.

39

Next, embroider the small fish using the same techniques as the large fish. Start by completing the outer contour with the split stitch.

40

Start from the tail and use the long and short stitch inside the fish body with thread 149 in red purple. When using the long and short stitch, gradually wrap around the outer contour line.

41

Gradually introduce thread 125 in brown red in the middle section.

42

Add thread 606 as transition and then 604 in medium purple at the fish head.

43

The fish body is completed. Here I turn the fabric in a clockwise direction.

44

Use the fly stitch to embroider the fish tail.

45

You can add dark colored threads near the part where the fish tail meets the fins.

46

Complete the left and right fins.

The small fish is now complete.

The overall effect after embroidering both fish.

Now, nail the beads as eyes for the large fish.

Thread the thinnest beading needle or sewing needle with black thread, come out from the head of the fish, and insert it into the middle of the bead.

Wrap around the bead from various angles for 3 to 4 stitches until the bead is completely secured and doesn't move.

Use the same method to secure the eye on the other side.

The eyes for the large fish are complete.

Complete the eyes for the small fish using the same method.

55

You can also use the same beads to add some embellishments to the flower's center.

56

Look at the completed image and see where it needs embellishments. At this point, you may add some variations to the middle trellis stitch.

57

Use thread 697 in brown to selectively fill in some of the interior spaces.

58

You can add a few stitches to the coral stitch of the outline to complement it. The placement of these stitches can be decided based on your preference or by referring to the finished image.

59

Partial details after completion.

60

The work is complete.

CHAPTER THREE
A Bite of Sweet Plant

Known for its slowness, the tortoise is also renowned for its longevity and has been considered an auspicious creature by the Chinese people from ancient times. Many of the famous oracle bone inscriptions are mostly inscribed on the plastron and carapace of tortoises, providing us with important historical materials for research and witnessing the origin and development of Chinese characters.

Shepherd's purse also has a long history of culinary use. It is said in the *Book of Songs*, "The taste of shepherd's purse is slightly bitter at first, but the aftertaste is sweet." Shepherd's purse grows widely throughout China and has a delicious flavor. Despite its humble appearance, it is beloved by people, much like the gentle, docile nature of the tortoise.

In this chapter, the tortoise and shepherd's purse are depicted with simple stitches and only two-color tones. The composition leans toward simplicity and elegance, aiming to capture the humble characteristics of the tortoise and shepherd's purse, and to showcase the diversity of wool embroidery. In the previous chapter, we used colorful floating heart to depict richness and beauty. In this chapter, we demonstrate how to use simple colors and stitches to portray the everyday joy of warmth and gentleness.

Preparatory Work

Before we begin, let's add some details about the embroidery base, specifically the fabric used for embroidery. In the second chapter, we briefly discussed the selection of fabric but did not mention how to determine its size. Considering that some beginners may not have a concept of this, additional information will be provided here.

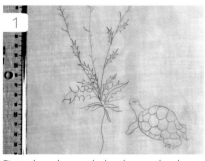

First, place the rough sketch onto the chosen fabric for embroidery and use a ruler to mark the length and width of the pattern.

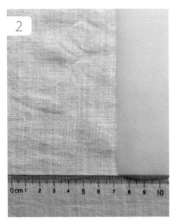

Then, add an additional 7 cm to both ends of the length and width measurements. This will be the final size required for the embroidery base. For example, if the pattern is 30 cm long and 21 cm wide, the embroidery base size would be 44 (length) × 35 (width) cm.

Before starting the embroidery, refer to the preparatory work from the previous chapter and transfer the design onto the fabric. You can use a water soluble pen to supplement any unclear parts of the transfer.

Prepare the required embroidery threads. You can also prepare two additional sets of threads in other colors according to your own needs.

5

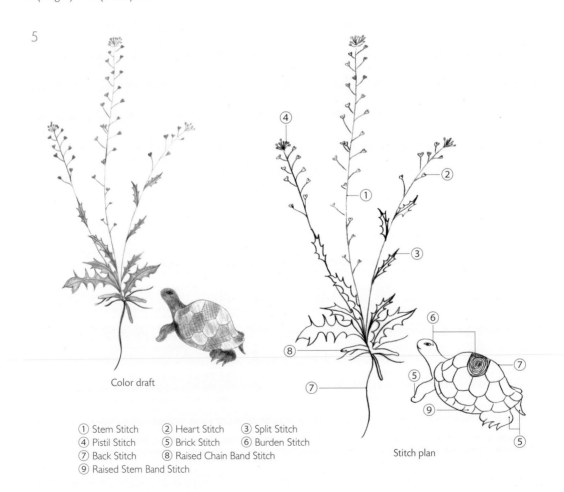

Color draft

Stitch plan

① Stem Stitch   ② Heart Stitch   ③ Split Stitch
④ Pistil Stitch   ⑤ Brick Stitch   ⑥ Burden Stitch
⑦ Back Stitch   ⑧ Raised Chain Band Stitch
⑨ Raised Stem Band Stitch

Confirm the stitch plan and the color draft.

Stitching Steps

In terms of composition, this tutorial does not adhere to the traditional Western wool embroidery style, but leans more towards the Chinese traditional meticulous painting style. Therefore, the stitching is simplified, focusing on the burden stitch of the tortoise shell, supplemented by several classic wool embroidery stitches such as the back stitch, stem stitch, etc., to create a refreshing and elegant atmosphere.

Tortoise

🧶 Burden Stitch

This stitching technique stands out in wool embroidery, using horizontal lines as the base and covering them with vertical lines to create a woven effect, imparting a unique aesthetic charm.

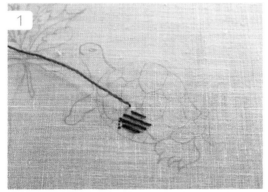

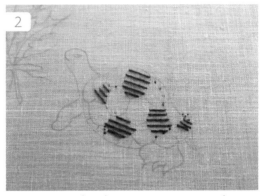

Begin the first stitching technique. As shown in the image, use thread 698 to create parallel lines with approximately 4 mm spacing within the small sections of the tortoise shell.

Continue to stitch in the same manner, spacing the rest of the sections of the shell. After completing one section, use the three stitch technique to directly stitch into another section to continue. Avoid pulling the thread directly on the backside, as it may cause snagging when stitching in the future.

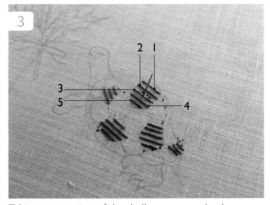

Taking one section of the shell as an example, there are a total of five horizontal lines within the section. For ease of explanation, we will use numbers 1 through 5 to represent the five lines from top to bottom. Use thread 915 to diagonally stitch out from above the midpoint of the third line.

Insert the needle at the midpoint below the first line.

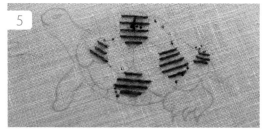

As shown in the picture, complete the first stitch, ensuring it remains perpendicular to the horizontal lines.

The second stitch is equivalent to shifting the first thread upwards. Stitch out from above the second horizontal line, then insert the needle from the top contour line. Repeat steps 3 to 6, alternating up and down, to the left.

After completing the left half, proceed to embroider the right half. While stitching, you can stabilize the thread with your left hand to ensure that each stitch is perpendicular to the horizontal lines.

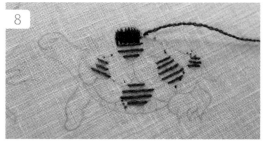

The picture shows the completed effect of the upper half of the shell section.

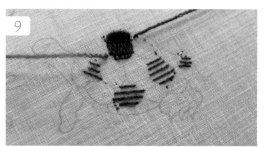

Switch to a lighter thread, number 913, and continue embroidering the lower half of the shell section. For this size of section, you can also alternate between three gradient shades (such as threads 698, 915, and 913).

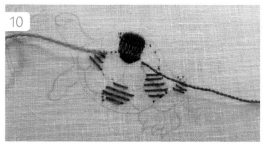

Fill the entire shell section. For the bottom part of the section, use thread 698.

After completing the first shell section, you can use the three stitch technique to stitch the remaining thread to the next pre-positioned shell section to continue embroidering. The picture shows the five completed shell sections.

After completing the first batch of shell sections, we will begin embroidering the remaining ones.

For the distribution of colors, if the first batch of shell sections is based on thread 903 with embroidery using threads 913 and 915, then the second batch of shell sections can be based on thread 913 with embroidery using threads 915 and 698. Here, we vary the combination of threads 913, 903, 915, and 698. This way, although the entire shell is within the same color range, there are subtle variations, making the image appear richer. The picture on the right shows a comparison of two different color schemes.

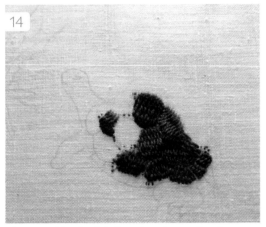

The second batch of shell sections is completed.

For the third set, you can use thread 915 as the base, and embroider using threads 903 and 913.

Upon close inspection, the stitching details resemble the texture of woven baskets.

Repeat the above steps, and the entire tortoise shell will be embroidered, presenting different layers of color through one stitching technique.

🪡 Brick Stitch

Brick stitch and burden stitch are very similar, with the main difference being that in brick stitch, the initial foundation is drawn with a pen rather than using thread, resulting in a slightly flatter appearance compared to the burden stitch.

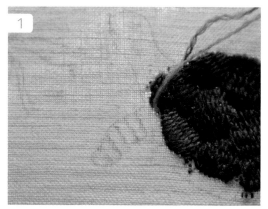

Use a ruler and a water soluble pen to draw lines spaced approximately 5 mm apart on the tortoise's forefoot.

Draw the interval lines on the rear foot in the same manner.

As with the burden stitch, maintain vertical stitching direction.

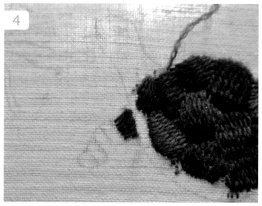

For the grid closest to the tortoise's body, use thread 915, the darkest brown color.

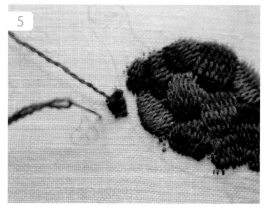

Continue embroidering with thread 915 on the next grid.

The effect after stitching the first two grids with thread lines.

Embroider the middle grid with thread 913, and complete the last two grids with thread 903 to finish the stitching for the front foot.

Apply the same stitching technique to the tortoise's rear foot.

The effect of completing the upper half with thread 915 is as shown in the picture. Here, three layers of stitches are embroidered from top to bottom, with the first layer of stitches being very short. Each layer of stitches is staggered and parallel to each other.

When stitching up to the tortoise's claw, use the split stitch with two to three stitches.

The completed effect of the tortoise's rear foot is as shown in the picture.

Returning to the tortoise's head, continue using the burden stitch to embroider.

The tortoise's head is brighter than its shell. Use thread 698 as the base and embroider the first row of vertical lines, then switch to thread 903.

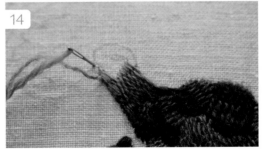

For the part near the top of the head, start by embroidering the lower jaw with thread 903.

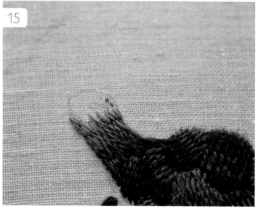

The image shows the completed effect of the lower jaw.

Complete the top part using the same thread and stitching technique.

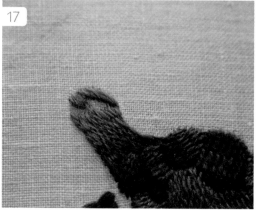

Don't forget to leave space for the mouth and eye.

Prepare DMC number 597 dark blue cotton thread. Each strand of DMC thread has six strands. Here, use two strands for embroidery. If DMC thread is not available, you can use thread from other brands as a substitute, and the thread color can also be changed to black.

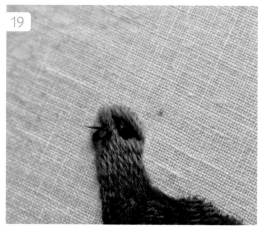

Use the stem stitch (refer to page 63) to complete the mouth and eye sections.

The completed effect of the eye and mouth. Use the brick stitch with threads 915 and 698 to embroider the tail.

🧶 Raised Stem Band Stitch

This stitching technique is a weaving style stitch in wool embroidery. Aside from the initial thread that needs to be pierced into the fabric, the rest of the stitching follows along the fabric surface.

To embroider the tortoise's plastron, first stitch vertical lines perpendicular to the tortoise shell using thread 698 as shown in the picture.

Switch to a size 22 tapestry needle. Starting just below the tortoise's neck, bring the needle out, then loop the needle around the first vertical line from right to left.

Pull tight and continue looping around the second vertical line.

Continue this process repeatedly until you loop around the last vertical line. Once you reach the right end of the plastron, end with the three stitch technique, but do not cut the thread.

Loop the thread from the right end to the leftmost vertical line, repeat steps 2 to 4 from right to left.

Once you reach the far left end, repeat steps 2 to 4 from left to right again. The picture shows the result after stitching the three rows of lines.

At this point, you may notice some areas with gaps. Use thread of a similar color and straight stitch to fill in these areas.

Use small stitches to fill in the gaps at the tortoise's shell and feet, ensuring there are no blank spaces.

With that, the entire tortoise is now complete.

Shepherd's Purse

🧶 Stem Stitch

The stem stitch technique, commonly used to depict the branches of trees, involves advancing one stitch forward and returning half a stitch to create a twisted rope-like appearance. It is similar to the split stitch, but it doesn't need to pass through the middle of the previous stitch when returning.

Use stem stitch with thread 833 to embroider the stems of the plant.

As shown in the picture, after stitching a short distance, come back to the middle of the previous two stitches and bring the needle out, continuing in the same manner.

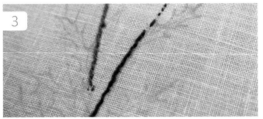

You can freely choose two different shades of green to embroider the two flower stems, such as thread 834 or 835.

For the leaf sections, use the split stitch (refer to page 43), but note that here, it requires shorter stitches.

As shown in the picture, keep each stitch within 5 mm.

Note that shepherd's purse leaves are coarse and have pointed edges, so finer stitches should be used to depict the details.

When encountering corners, it is important to preserve the characteristic pointed edges of shepherd's purse leaves.

The lower outline of the leaf section is completed.

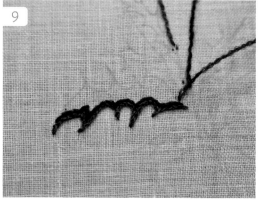

Use the dark green thread 835 with a split stitch to embroider the second layer of outline along the first layer's contour line.

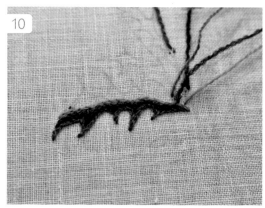

Embroider the central vein of the leaf using the lightest green thread 403, with the split stitch.

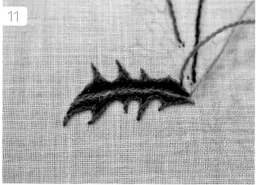

Complete the upper half of the leaf in the same manner. The finished effect of the entire leaf is as shown in the picture.

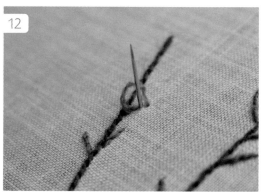

Use the stem stitch with thread 403 to embroider the small branches on both sides of the flower stem.

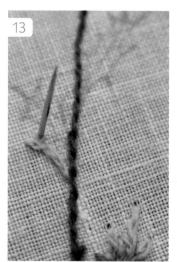

Continue using the split stitch, flexibly applying different shades of green to embroider the other leaves. In the image, thread 431 is used to embroider the leaves.

The completed effect of the shepherd's purse leaves and stems.

As shown in the picture, you can also add more decorative details to the leaves according to your personal preference.

🧶 Heart Stitch

I will use a custom stitching technique to embroider the shepherd's purse fruits. Shepherd's purse fruits resemble flattened green hearts, so I call this stitching technique the "heart stitch," which is derived from the fishbone stitch.

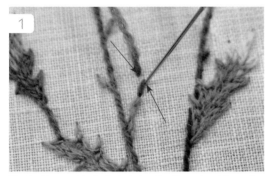

Start with a vertical stitch, bring the thread out from the top left corner (as indicated by the red arrow), and then insert the needle on the right side of the vertical stitch (as indicated by the blue arrow).

Next, bring the needle out from the top right corner (as indicated by the red arrow), then insert it on the left side of the top of the vertical stitch.

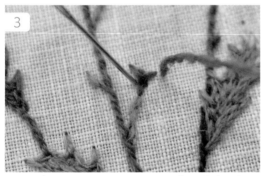

Repeat this process, continuing to stitch in a left-right alternating pattern. Each left and right stitch pair counts as one set.

After completing approximately four or five sets of stitches, one small green heart shape is completed.

Using the same method, embroider another small heart shape. When finishing one heart, you can hide the stitches under the stem, as shown in the picture. Then, on the back of the fabric, bring the thread forward to the next small heart to be embroidered.

🌀 Pistil Stitch

The pistil stitch can be used not only to embroider flower pistils but also to embroider antennae for butterflies and other small insects.

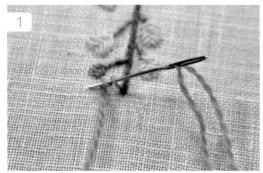

For better visibility, display the stitching technique with the fabric turned over. Use thread 403 to bring the needle out at the top of the stem. With the right hand holding the needle, wrap the thread around two to three times with the left hand, then insert the needle into the fabric at a certain distance away from the stem.

After pulling the thread tight with the left hand, fully insert the needle into the fabric, pulling the thread to the back of the fabric.

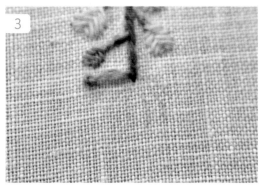

One small completed pistil stitch.

Continue embroidering the pistil stitches in the same manner.

You can depict the stamen section using two different colors, which adds more richness. Here, use threads 403 and 551.

🧶 Back Stitch

This is the most basic stitch in wool embroidery. The method is to take two steps forward and one step back, giving the stitch its name.

For the roots of the plant, use thread 915. Start with the most basic embroidery stitch, the back stitch. Begin by bringing the needle out for the first stitch (point A), then after a short distance, insert it for the second (point B).

The third stitch (point C) comes out at a position equal to the distance between the first and second stitches, then goes back to the position of the second stitch (point B), forming a back stitch.

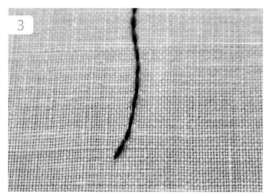

Continue repeating steps 1 and 2. The result is as shown in the picture.

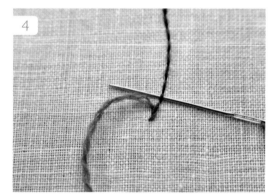

Take a size 22 tapestry needle. As shown in the picture, switch to thread 698 in the same color range, but a different shade. Wrap the first stitch from right to left. Repeat steps 1 to 4 to embroider the other rhizomes.

In this way, embroider five different lengths of bicolored threads to complete the root of the shepherd's purse.

🐚 Raised Chain Band Stitch

Like raised stem band stitch, this is a technique primarily based on wrapping thread around previously laid horizontal lines using a needle.

Use thread 698 to embroider three thicker rhizomes, taking the middle one as an example. First, work a row of small horizontal stitches from bottom to top, then bring the needle out from the top after completing them.

Insert the needle from below the first horizontal line, with the needle pointing toward the upper left corner.

Pull the thread tight, then insert the needle from the upper right corner back into the first horizontal line, with the needle pointing toward the lower left corner. Note that the needle should press down on the thread at this point.

After pulling tight, a knot is formed.

Repeat steps 2 to 4 to wrap the horizontal stitches below one by one.

Ensure that tension is maintained on each stitch.

As shown in the picture, repeat the stitching process to form a series of knots.

When reaching the second to last stitch, insert the needle directly to the back.

For the last stitch, pass the needle through the previous stitch to form a back stitch.

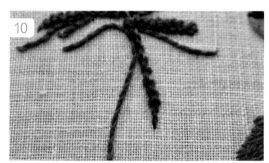

Make one more stitch forward to form a small tail, then insert the needle into the fabric to finish. This outlines a thicker rhizome.

The piece is complete.

The other two thicker rhizomes are also embroidered in the same way (as shown by the red arrows).

CHAPTER FOUR
Envying the Love of Mandarin Ducks

Pine needles are different from the leaves of other trees: they are stiff and strong, and when collected and ignited, they give off a special fragrance. Pine trees are also used for afforestation in barren mountains. They are valuable in many ways, as their needles can be boiled for medicinal use, and pine resin can be extracted for turpentine. In fertile soil, pine trees can grow into towering giants, but in steep valleys and cliffs, they twist and turn, earning them the poetic description among the literati: *branches like wandering dragons, leaves like soaring phoenixes.*

There is a passage in the classic Chinese love poem *The Peacock Flies Southeast* that reads, "In east and west stand pines and cypresses, while to the left and right grow parasol trees. Branches interlace with each other, and leaves intertwine in communication. In between, a pair of flying birds, calling themselves mandarin ducks. Facing each other, they sing, every night until the fifth watch." Pines symbolize longevity and immortality, while mandarin ducks symbolize love. Pine tree and mandarin ducks are the main focus of this chapter.

Preparatory Work

As a beginning to this chapter, do not rush into embroidering, but instead start by dyeing the fabric. Of course, if you find it troublesome and have ready-made dark fabric, you can skip this step. Because the crewelwork fabric (The Crewelwork Company brand) used for embroidery in this chapter only comes in one color officially, so we will use it to demonstrate how to dye the fabric.

Start by mixing black acrylic or watercolor paint, then add a large amount of white paint to achieve a dark gray color. Dilute with 5 to 10 ml of water, then use a flat acrylic brush to apply paint to one corner of the embroidery fabric. Match the color to that shown in the picture.

After testing the color, start applying it to the fabric, beginning in the center and expanding outward. Since the fabric is initially completely dry, the color will be absorbed quickly with the first few strokes.

After applying the first layer of color, you may notice some white spots showing through the fabric. This is normal. Simply continue adding a second or third layer of color until the desired depth is achieved.

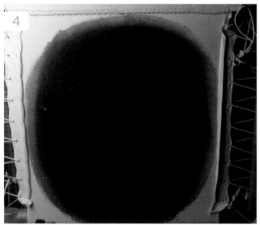

For the fourth layer of color, I added some dark green to the original dark gray, diluted it with water, and achieved the final color effect as shown in the picture.

Once the fabric is completely dry, proceed with the tracing of the pattern.

Here, I used green transfer paper. I left the pine needles and the feathers around the neck of the mandarin ducks blank for now, without tracing them.

For this embroidery project, I have prepared five color tones with fifteen different thread colors. You can also add other colors as needed during the embroidery process.

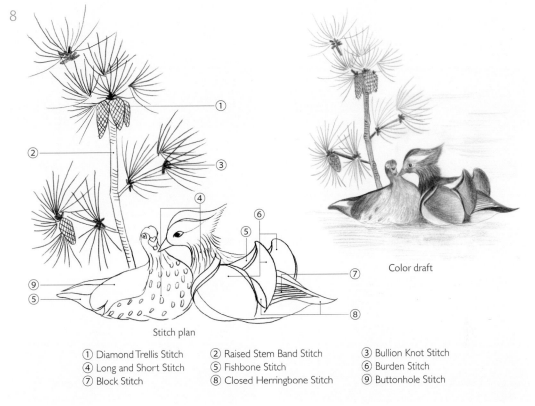

8

① Diamond Trellis Stitch
④ Long and Short Stitch
⑦ Block Stitch

② Raised Stem Band Stitch
⑤ Fishbone Stitch
⑧ Closed Herringbone Stitch

③ Bullion Knot Stitch
⑥ Burden Stitch
⑨ Buttonhole Stitch

Stitch plan

Color draft

Prepare the stitch plan and the color draft. (*Because of the intricacy of bird feathers, the stitch plan does not list all stitches, please refer to steps for more details.)

Stitching Steps

In this tutorial case, we will primarily use the long and short stitch, incorporating new stitches such as closed herringbone stitch and bullion knot stitch, and reviewing previously learned stitches such as fishbone stitch and burden stitch.

Mandarin Ducks

🧶 Burden Stitch

First, review the stitches learned in chapter two. Start by stitching parallel lines spaced approximately 4 mm apart using thread 854.

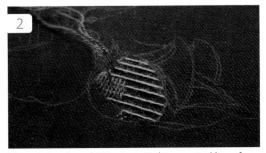

Then, using thread 478, start stitching vertical lines from the left side.

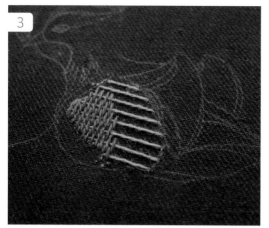

3

For the mandarin ducks' feathers in this section, there is a gradient from left to right. When stitching up to this point, you will need to switch to a different color.

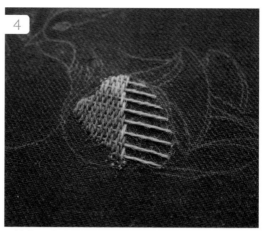

4

Add thread 854, which is the same color as the base parallel lines, to stitch the lines.

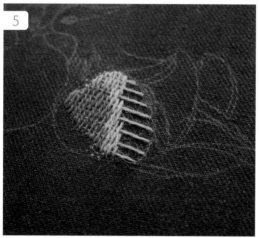

5

Start from the top left and gradually stitch down to the bottom right.

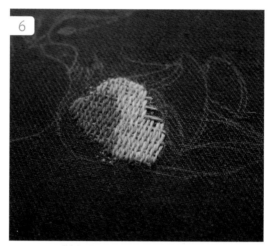

6

Leave a small blank space when nearing the end.

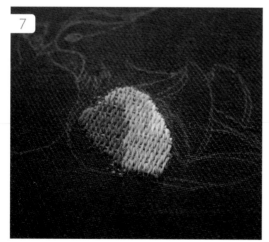

7

Add thread 705 to brighten the colors.

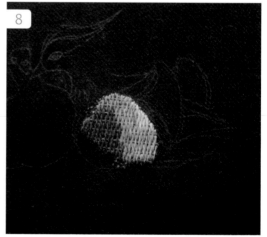

8

Check the overall effect from a distance to see if any adjustments are needed.

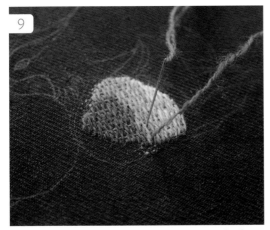

If you feel there is a lack of transition between the first and second colors, you can add an intermediate color, thread 914.

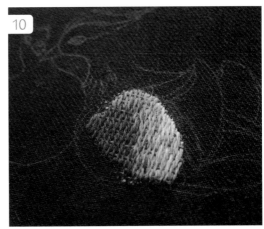

Only add five or six stitches to gently blend the border.

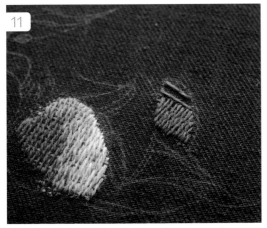

Continue stitching the wing on the back using the same method as before. Start by stitching parallel lines with thread 914, then fill in with vertical lines.

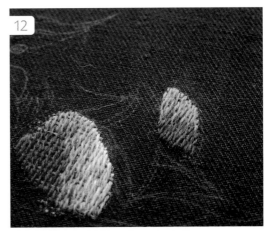

Then, add thread 854 to the upper half.

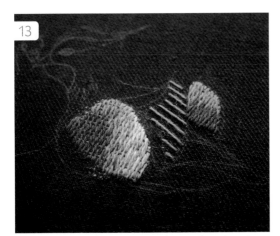

Continue embroidering the wing in the front. Start by stitching parallel lines with thread 477.

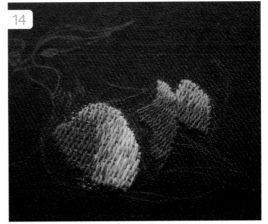

For this part, use the three colors previously used to construct the gradient from dark to light, starting from the bottom up: threads 478, 914, and 854.

🧶 Block Stitch

This requires a highly precise technique and layering. Begin with a split stitch as the base, then overlay with a satin stitch.

Start by bringing the needle up using the three stitch technique with thread 991b, then work split stitch from left to right. (Because of author's embroidery order, one black feather is already shown here, and you will see its tutorial later.)

After completing a section of the split stitch, work back diagonally from the end of the white line. Bring the needle up from the lower left side of the white line and insert it on the upper right side.

Each stitch should be close together, so that there are no gaps. As shown in the image, each segment of satin stitch from right to left is slightly longer than the previous one.

The picture shows the completed first layer of white feathers. Steps 1 to 4 constitute one block stitch.

To embroider the second layer of white feathers, follow the same method as before, starting with a row of split stitch.

Repeat steps 2 to 4 to complete the second block stitch.

Finally, complete the third layer of white feathers using the same method.

After completing the three layers, take pine green thread 528 to add some details.

At the intervals between the three layers of feathers, use the stem stitch.

Ensure that each stitch falls between the intervals of the two white feathers.

Complete two rows of stem stitch in this manner.

The final two layers of pine green and gray black (as indicated by the red arrow) are completed using block stitch. The gray black feather on the left (as indicated by the green arrow) is embroidered using closed herringbone stitch (see the next section for the technique).

🧶 Closed Herringbone Stitch

The herringbone and fishbone stitches are both types of fishbone embroidery. The difference lies in where the needle enters the fabric. In the closed herringbone stitch, it enters on either side of the fishbone, while in the fishbone stitch, it enters along the center line of the fishbone. The closed herringbone stitch thus produces a denser effect.

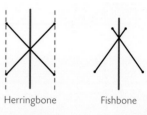

Herringbone   Fishbone

Take thread 489 and start stitching from the position indicated in the picture, entering along the center line to create a vertical line.

Bring the needle out from the left side at the top of the vertical line.

The entry point for the needle is located on the upper right side of the vertical line.

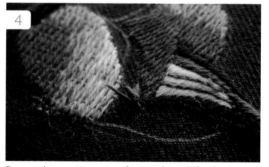

Repeat the previous steps from right to left. That is, bring the needle out from the right side at the top of the vertical line, then insert it on the left side of the vertical line.

Continue stitching in the same manner.

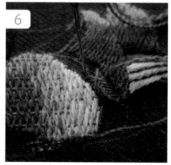

The picture shows the effect of the stitching up to the middle section.

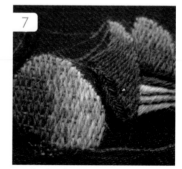

Finally, finish off with the three stitch technique to complete a full closed herringbone stitch.

🧶 Fishbone Stitch

For the next feather, use the fishbone stitch to create detail contrast with the closed herringbone stitch.

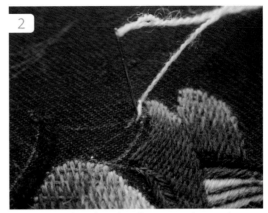

With embroidery thread 991b, start stitching with the three stitch technique from the top. Begin with a straight stitch, then exit on the upper right and enter on the lower left.

Then exit on the upper left, enter on the lower right, and continue alternating between left and right until reaching the middle section.

Here, I deliberately present the white feather slightly looser than the previous blue feather, showcasing the subtle differences in stitch detail within the same series.

Continuing with the remaining thread, as shown by the red arrow, use the split stitch to outline a section of the design.

Use the block stitch with thread 621 to wrap around.

Using thread 588, fill in the remaining gaps between the white feather and the blue feather with block stitch. Then, use fishbone stitch and closed herringbone stitch to complete the feathers at the neck and tail sections (as shown by the red arrows).

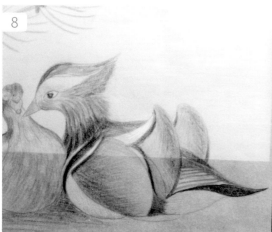

With the stitching completed up to this point, compare the color draft with the parts that have already been finished.

For the small feather at the top, use the fishbone stitch, alternating between embroidery threads 955 and 766 to achieve a two-color effect.

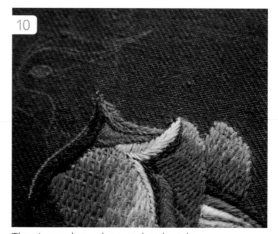

The picture shows the completed result.

⬡ General Application of Stitching Techniques
From this point onward, we will integrate the previously learned stitch techniques.

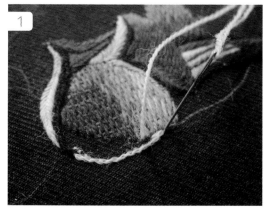

Embroider a tuft of white feathers below the mandarin duck's neck using fishbone stitch with embroidery thread 991b. Then, use split stitch to embroider the outline of the abdomen.

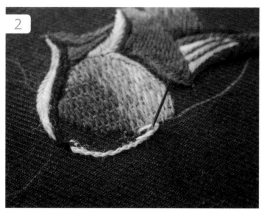

Starting from the right tip, use the long and short stitch to continue embroidering.

Slowly wrap stitches from the outside towards the inside (similar to the block stitch on page 76 in method), enveloping the outline created in step 1.

You can also wrap stitches from the inside towards the outside. With proficiency in any stitching technique, you can be flexible and adapt as needed.

Continue embroidering inward using the long and short stitch. The long and short stitch is an essential basic technique commonly used in crewel embroidery, so it is worth practicing and mastering.

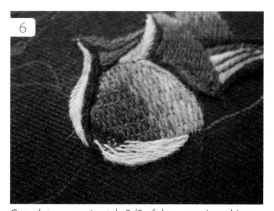

Complete approximately 2/3 of the area using white thread 991b.

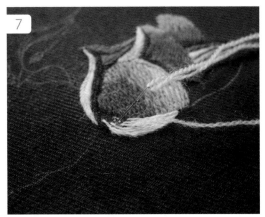

7

Incorporate pink thread 621.

8

Continue using the long and short stitch technique, ensuring accurate angles while stitching along the direction of the mandarin duck's feathers. Keep the stitches relatively short.

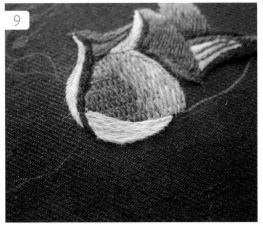

9

The completed effect of the abdomen is shown in the picture.

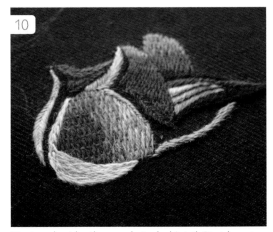

10

Next, embroider the mandarin duck's tail. Start by using thread 525 to create an outline with split stitch, then wrap the split stitch obliquely.

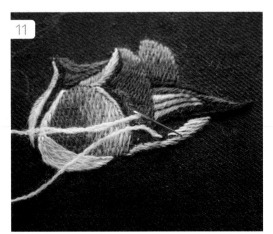

11

Embroider diagonally with thread 991b, leaving a slight gap between each row of white stitches for the next row.

12

Fill in the blank spaces with long and short stitch using white thread.

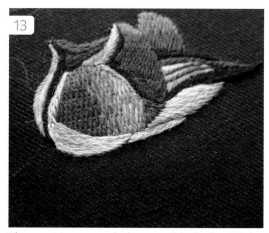

The remaining area at the bottom of the body is filled using the long and short stitch technique in thread 877.

Next, embroider the head. Use closed herringbone stitch and thread 854 to embroider the feather on the top of the head.

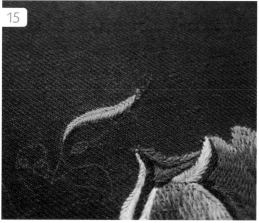

Here, a single-colored thread is used, but for more detailed work, you could also use gradient thread, transitioning from dark to light.

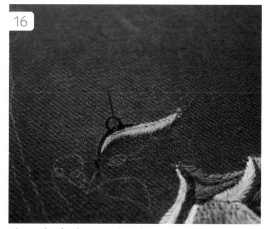

Above this feather, use thread 588 to create a row of stem stitch along the edge.

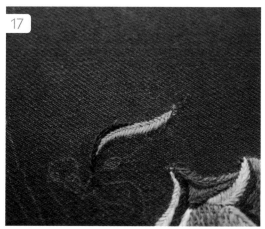

Stitch this layer only until it reaches the middle section of the first layer.

Start detailing with the face. Use white thread 991b with the long and short stitch technique, employing tiny short stitches for the eye socket.

Gradually incorporate pink thread 621 and continue embroidering with the long and short stitch technique until reaching the space above the eye socket.

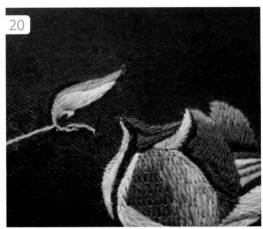

Using the same technique, continue with thread 862, a pink orange color, outlining the left side of the eye socket, then proceed toward the neck.

At the neck, use split stitch to create spaced lines resembling a series of chains.

Fill the spaces with thread 588 between the chains and the back of the neck in split stitch, as shown in the picture. Continue with split stitch toward the upper right side of the head.

Ensure that the stitching is evenly spaced and well balanced.

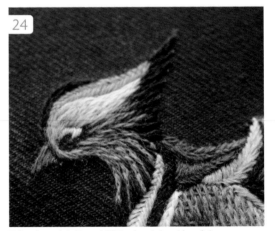

Take thread 862 and fill in the right side of the eye socket as shown in the picture. Then, embroider 45-degree diagonal lines to form the base for the beak.

On top of the base you've created, continue using thread 862 to wrap another layer of stitches in the opposite 45-degree direction.

After wrapping the beak, continue filling the right side of the eye socket using thread 862 and a small amount of thread 914, employing the long and short stitch technique.

Prepare to fill in the details of the eye.

Take a small section of thread 588 and separate it into two strands, then switch to a size 24 chenille needle.

Use thread 993 to fill in the eyeball with parallel short stitches, some of which may cover the previously completed white embroidery. Then, use stem stitch to embroider the outline of the eye socket.

At this point, the male mandarin duck is complete.

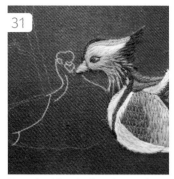

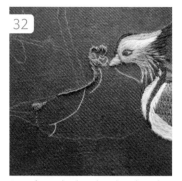

To embroider the female mandarin duck, as shown in the picture, start by outlining the dividing lines using a water soluble pen.

Start from the head and embroider a section of stem stitches using thread 567 along the back. Near the cheeks, you can embroider a few short stitches. Then, embroider a small fishbone stitch at the tail.

As shown in the picture, first make a few diagonal stitches on the left side of the head with thread 588. Then, take thread 698, a brown color, and add details to the head with short stitches. Ensure that the stitches are small.

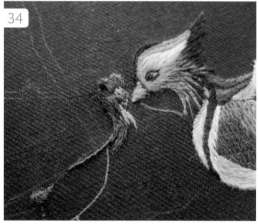

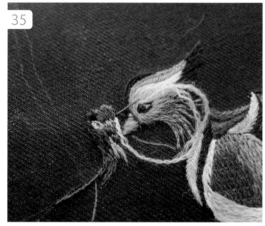

Then, on top of the stitches made with thread 698, add pink orange thread 862, leaving space for the eye socket (as indicated by the red arrow).

Use white thread 991b to outline the left eye using stem stitch technique. For the right eye, only two small stitches are needed.

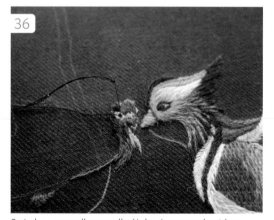

Switch to a smaller needle (John James embroidery needle size 9 is used here) and use single strand black cotton thread DMC No. 310 to add details to the eye using running stitch.

The details of the head are complete.

Continue stitching downward from the neck with white thread 991b, using the long and short stitch technique.

Incorporate light brown thread 912, aiming to enter the stitches at a 45-degree angle for a smooth transition.

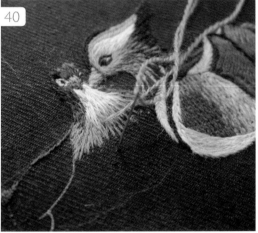

The light brown thread 912 runs approximately to the middle of the chest.

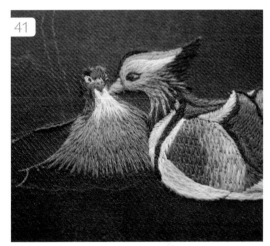

Add thread 766.

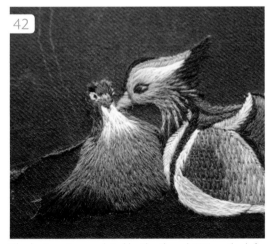

The bottom is completed by the thread 588 on the left side and the deep brown thread 955 on the right side.

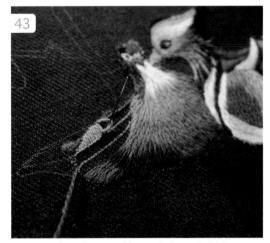

Next, use thread 302 and buttonhole stitch (refer to page 36) to embroider the wing of the mandarin duck.

Work from left to right, maintaining consistent spacing between each stitch as much as possible.

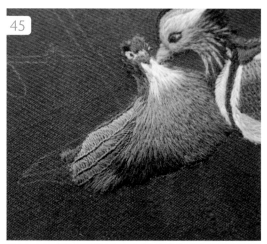

The second row of feathers is embroidered in thread 766, and the third row in thread 955.

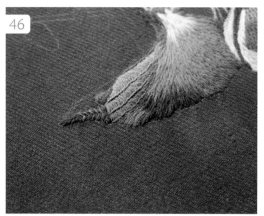

The long feathers at the tail are embroidered using fishbone stitch technique, primarily with thread 588, accented with several strands of thread 955.

Add another row of fishbone stitches on top of the tail. Returning to the chest area, use split stitch with thread 862 to add bright details. Each small dot requires only two to three stitches.

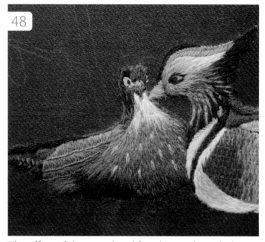

The effect of the completed female mandarin duck.

Two mandarin ducks are complete.

Pine Tree

🧶 General Application of Stitching Techniques

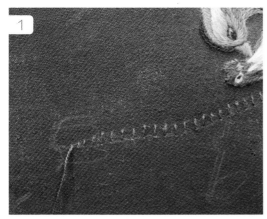

Use the raised stem band stitch to embroider the trunk of the pine tree. Start by stitching a row of short vertical lines from right to left using thread 955.

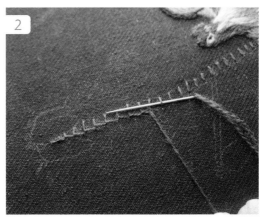

Switch to a tapestry needle, and from left to right, use thread 955 to wrap around the vertical lines as shown in the picture.

For the final stitch, pierce directly to the back of the fabric, then use the three stitch technique to finish.

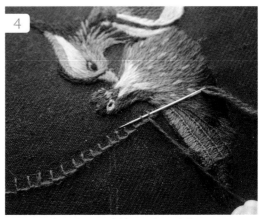

Wrap the thread around from right to left once more.

After completing the two rows of thread, add thread 588 and continue wrapping to create a sense of depth and texture.

Once finished, use the three stitch technique to hide the needle stitches on the side.

Go back to the base, between the mandarin duck and the branch, add some details using the long and short stitch (as shown by the red arrow).

Embroider small branches using stem stitch.

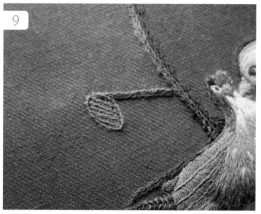

Next, move on to the pinecone part. You may want to review the diamond trellis stitch (refer to page 27). First, create a layer of grids in the center using thread 955, then proceed to outline it with a round of back stitches.

Use thread 588 to anchor all the intersections within the pinecone, then wrap the thread around the back stitch outline.

Next, use a new stitch, the bullion knot stitch. Start by pulling out the needle and thread approximately 4 mm away from the top of the pinecone.

Then, insert the needle at the top of the pinecone and come out at the same point where previous stitch exits, leaving approximately 1 cm of the needle shaft exposed, as shown in the picture.

Start wrapping the thread tightly around the needle, with the loops closely arranged.

After wrapping approximately seven to eight loops, secure the loops with your left hand and push the needle through with your right hand.

After pushing the needle completely through the loops, use it to rearrange the loops, stacking them neatly.

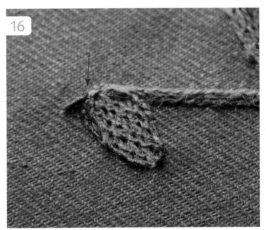

Insert the needle directly from the top of the pinecone (as indicated by the red arrow) and bring it to the back of the fabric.

Repeat steps 11 to 16 to complete the remaining six bullion knots.

Finally, embroider the pine needles using back stitch with pine green thread 528.

When you reach the convergence point of the five pine needles, if there is excess thread, you can switch to a tapestry needle to wrap the pine needles on the fabric surface.

Some of the pine needles can be embroidered using gradient colors to enrich the effect.

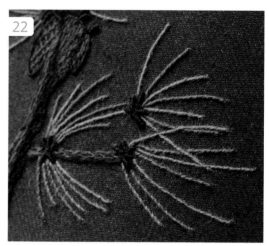

After completing all the pine needles, continue adding bullion knots at the intersections of the pine needles.

The finished effect of the pine needles.

Next, embroider three stacked pinecones (as shown by the red arrow) using the diamond trellis stitch.

For the grid section, use a slightly brighter thread 766 for the center pinecone and slightly darker thread 955 for the pinecones on the sides. Continue by nailing sesame to the center and right pinecones in thread 588 and to the left pinecone with thread 766.

When embroidering this part, you may notice that because the pinecones are relatively slender, the grids appear to be squeezed together, which also gives the pinecones a sense of texture and depth.

Here, I turn the diagram in step 25 clockwise. Embroider the outline of the pinecones using back stitch, then wrap thread along the outline.

The finished effect of the pinecones is as shown in the picture.

The work is complete.

CHAPTER FIVE
Before the Mulberry Leaves Fall

This piece embodies the most classic style of wool embroidery, mainly composed of geometric patterns with relatively fewer realistic elements. The dozen or so leaves in the work are embroidered with various stitching techniques, including those mentioned in previous cases and some new ones. I hope you will experience the pleasure of integrated stitching techniques through this piece.

The image contains elements such as mulberry leaves, mulberries, silkworms, and butterflies. Mulberry trees have a long history in China, with records dating back to oracle bones. They were revered as sacred trees for temple worship during the Shang and Zhou dynasties (1600–256 BC). The *Book of Songs* contains numerous poems related to mulberry trees, including descriptions of their appearance and scenes depicting women gathering mulberry leaves. In mythology and legend, there is a story of Nüwa scattering mulberry tree seeds, which bore mulberries, to alleviate famine among the people.

Where there is mulberry, there are silkworms, and subsequently, the Chinese invented the use of silkworm silk to produce beautiful fabrics. Clothing made of silk is exquisite and soft, and it has been popular all over the world.

Preparatory Work

Readers have already become familiar with the application of basic stitching techniques through the exercises in the previous three cases, so this project will not delve into them further. Because the perception of embroidery is also crucial throughout the entire learning process, this chapter will focus more on describing the details and sensations experienced during the embroidery process.

Begin by preparing fourteen colors of embroidery threads according to the color draft. As mentioned in the previous embroidery cases, although we prepare embroidery threads according to the color draft, colors can be adjusted and added or reduced during the embroidery process as needed. The same applies to the stitch plan.

After tracing the design, take a moment to review the prepared color draft and stitch plan. The draft on the right contrasts the color of the transfer paper (light colored ink) with the color of the water soluble pen (dark colored ink). In general, transfer paper produces clearer lines on smooth fabric compared to textured fabric. In this case, we are using professional wool embroidery fabric, and the traced lines from the transfer paper appear somewhat faint. However, in actual practice, as long as the traces are visible to the naked eye, it should be fine. If it is necessary to intensify the traced lines, you can use a water soluble pen to redraw the parts that need to be embroidered on that day. Since air humidity varies in different regions, the speed at which the marks from the water soluble pen disappear also varies, so it is advisable to redraw only the sections that will be embroidered.

3

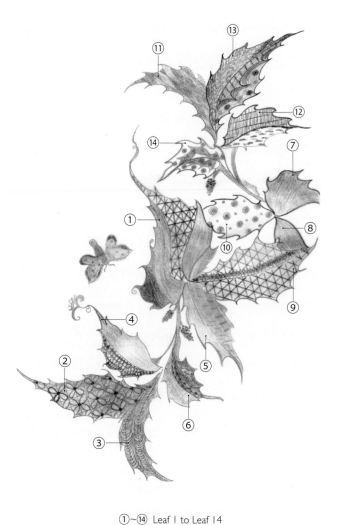

①~⑭ Leaf 1 to Leaf 14

Here, I mark the numbers on the leaves to facilitate subsequent embroidery.

Stitching Steps

This project combines various stitching techniques from the previous three chapters. To avoid repetition, apart from detailing new stitching techniques separately, the steps for other stitching techniques will be briefly hinted at or directly referenced to the pages where they were previously described.

Mulberry Leaves

🧶 Diamond Trellis Stitch

Begin with the diamond trellis stitch (refer to page 27) to embroider the central part of leaf 1 in the middle of the design.

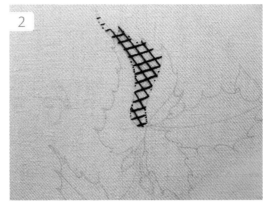

Use thread 998 as the base.

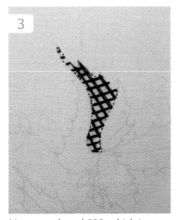

Next, use thread 588, which is a similar color, to embroider the second layer.

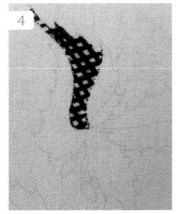

Add thread 716 for the third layer.

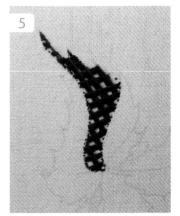

Finally, use thread 758 for the last layer.

In the beginner's case, we end by anchoring all the intersections at this point. This project introduces a small variation: add a row of parallel thread 716 stitches at each intersection point of the crimson thread 758.

Use thread 477 to anchor all the intersections to create a slightly modified diamond trellis stitch.

🧶 Long and Short Stitch

Next, we use the long and short stitch (refer to page 43) along with the pre-selected gradient thread to fill in the right side of this leaf.

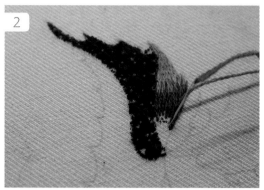

Because thread 854 at the tip of the leaf and thread 744 in the next layer belong to completely different color palettes, there will be some difficulty in the transition. The technique to handle this is to take a few long stitches at the transition point before transitioning to the next color layer. If you find it challenging to achieve the desired effect or if the transition is difficult to manage, you can also switch back to using the same color palette thread to embroider this part.

🧶 Chain Stitch

This is a technique in which a series of looped stitches form a chain-like pattern. It can be stitched along a curved or straight line.

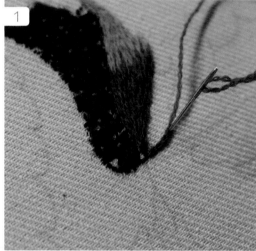

If there is excess thread after completing the long and short stitch with thread 489, you can continue by using the chain stitch to embroider the outline of the right side of the leaf. To begin the chain stitch, bring the needle up through the back of the fabric to the front at the beginning of the line to be worked. Take the needle down near the hole where the thread comes up, pull until it forms a small loop, and don't pull through yet. Bring the tip of the needle up a stitch distance away, and make it within the loop. Pull the needle through above the loop. Continue stitching in the same manner.

The second row of chain stitch on the left will be done using thread 567.

Then, fill the entire leaf segment from right to left using the chain stitch with threads 567, 744, and 489.

🧶 Raised Stem Band Stitch

Next, use the raised stem band stitch (refer to page 61) along with the pre-selected gradient thread to fill in the left side of leaf 1.

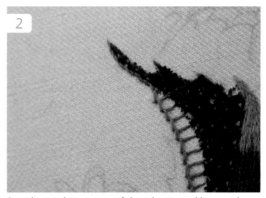

Start by stitching a row of short horizontal lines with thread 477, then wrap the thread from top to bottom around the stitches.

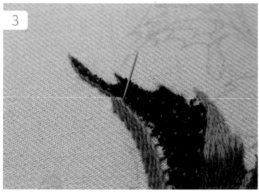

Wrap thread 477 around for three rows, then switch to thread 854 and continue wrapping around the stitches.

During the embroidery process, if you find it difficult to pull the needle out due to the angle, you can use tweezers to assist.

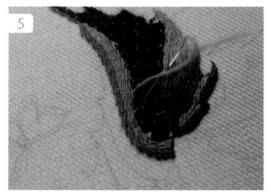

At the end, simply take the needle directly to the back side.

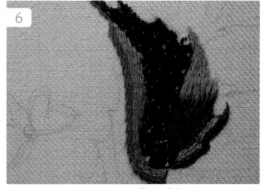

Compared to the wrapping effect of the pine tree trunk in chapter four (refer to page 89), the wrapping effect of this mulberry leaf segment appears denser. This is because, in addition to increasing the number of rows of wrapping, the wrapping sequence for each row is from top to bottom in the same direction. The pine tree trunk, on the other hand, wraps from top to bottom and then from bottom to top, creating natural gaps between each row.

Continue embroidering with thread 904 toward the left side.

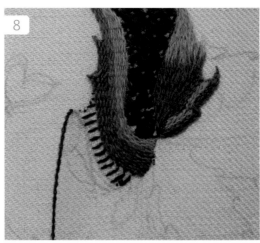

Add thread 716 to the left of 904 to complement the color in the middle of the leaf segment.

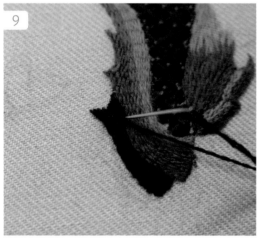

The picture shows the position to hide the needle at the end.

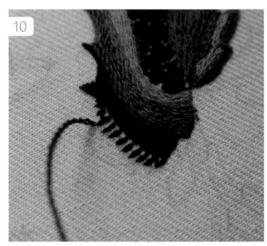

Continue stitching towards the left side with thread 588.

Finish embroidering the left side of the leaf with thread 998. This completes the multi-layered raised stem band stitch.

The detailed effect after completion is as shown in the picture.

◎ Laid Work Stitch

This technique is simply described as parallel stitching, commonly used to quickly fill small areas with color or as a base for larger color blocks. It can then be overlaid with trellis stitch or other stitching techniques.

We will use laid work stitch to embroider leaf 2.

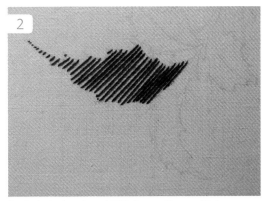

Begin by laying thread 998 diagonally at a 45-degree angle. The laying method should be similar to the grid pattern used in square trellis stitch as described in chapter two (refer to page 23).

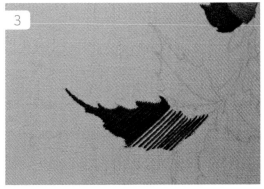

Using the middle of the leaf as a reference point, start by laying threads from the middle toward the left side. Then, from the left side back toward the middle, fill in the gaps left by the first pass of threads. This method helps to prevent the threads from becoming misaligned.

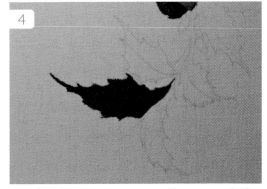

Complete the remaining part using the same method.

Then, use thread 716 to create grids, anchor all the intersections using thread 758, adding a layer of diamond trellis stitch.

🐚 Detached Chain Stitch

This stitching technique is adept at creating texture and quickly filling large areas of the embroidered surface.

Next, we will learn a new stitching technique called detached chain stitch, which is similar to the fly stitch (refer to page 46). The picture shows the finished effect.

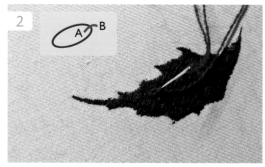

First, come up with the needle near the right side of the anchored intersection, then go back into the same spot to create a small loop. Then draw the needle from the inner center of the loop (refer to the diagram, point A), and finally, nail the thread tightly in the outer center of the loop (point B). This will produce a small petal.

Four small petals form one group, using threads 758, 716, and 904 with color coordination. Within this, you can also intersperse single or double petals.

🐚 Fly Stitch, Long and Short Stitch

Next, we will use the fly stitch (refer to step 23 on page 46) to embroider leaf 3 with a gradient orange color. Prepare three colors of wool threads.

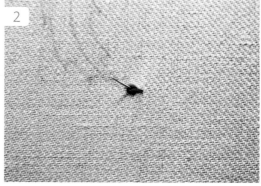

Using thread 904, start by stitching a stitch of about 4 mm at the top, then pull out the first loop and tighten it.

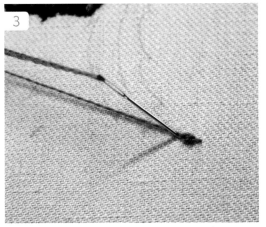

When securing the thread, maintaining a 45-degree angle while stitching will result in a more aesthetically pleasing appearance.

Gradually switch to thread 477.

Due to the shape, longer stitches may result in the embroidery not lying flat enough. We can use the split stitch (refer to page 43) to add 1 to 2 stitches in the middle of the thread, securing the thread in the desired position.

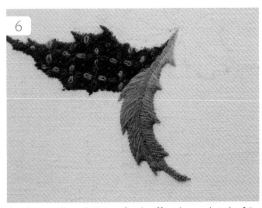

Finally, use thread 854 to finish off and complete leaf 3.

Next, in coordination with leaf 1, use threads 854, 744, and 567 along with the long and short stitch (refer to page 43) to embroider the right half of leaf 4.

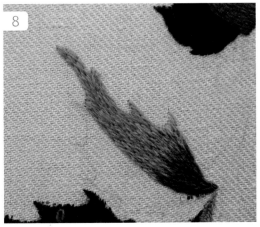

The detail after completion is as shown in the picture.

🧶 Coral Stitch, Long and Short Stitch

1

Next, use threads 854, 477, 904, and 998 along with the coral stitch (refer to page 33) to embroider the left half of leaf 4. Please note that double thread stitching will be used for this part.

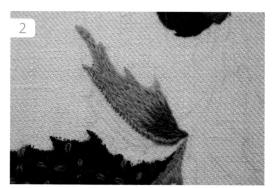

2

Start by stitching a row with thread 854.

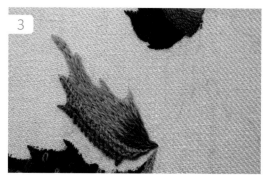

3

Then, use threads 477 and 904 to complete the second and third rows. Finally, fill in the remaining areas with thread 998.

4

Next, use the long and short stitch to complete the left side of leaf 5 with threads 845, 477, 904, and 998 in order from bottom to top.

🧶 Cretan Stitch

The cretan stitch is a clever, logically rigorous stitching technique, commonly used to build outlines or depict thicker leaf veins.

1

We will use a new stitching technique, cretan stitch, to embroider left half of leaf 6. Before stitching, draw two guidelines (A and B) in the center of the segment (between the left and the middle contour line).

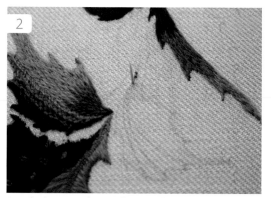

2

Start by bringing the needle out after applying three stitch technique at the base of the leaf segment.

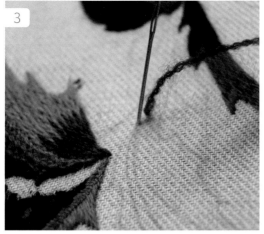

Make one stitch toward the left contour line.

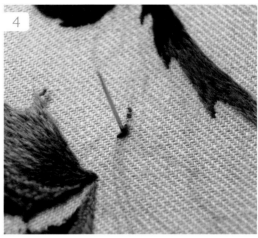

Come up above the midpoint of the previous stitch.

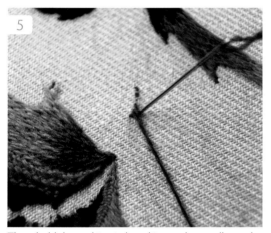

Then, hold down this stitch and insert the needle on the middle contour line.

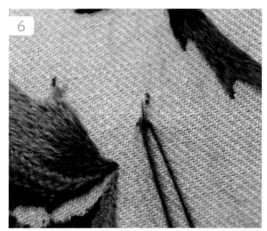

As shown in the picture, bring the needle out below the point where it entered (while holding down the left thread).

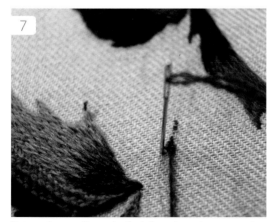

Return the needle to the far left and continue repeating steps 3 to 6. The only variation is that as the leaf widens gradually from top to bottom, you must keep the entry stitches along the contour of the leaf, while the exit stitches are made on the guidelines drawn.

From this picture, it is evident that the entry stitch is made on the left contour line.

The exit point is on the guideline drawn (line A).

Similarly, continue by entering the needle from the middle contour line.

Pull the needle out from the second guideline (line B) on the inner side.

You will notice that the cretan stitch is somewhat like a drifting fly stitch from left to right.

The picture shows the completed effect of the entire leaf segment. For the last few stitches near the leaf tip, simply fill in the blank spaces with parallel stitches.

🧶 Stem Stitch, Long and Short Stitch

Use stem stitch (refer to page 63) to complete the right half of leaf 6. As shown in the picture, we will use three distinct color blocks to complete this segment. The threads from right to left are 904, 403, and 834.

For the two small leaves (leaf 7 and leaf 8), we will continue using the long and short stitch, which requires plenty of practice, since it is the most commonly used stitching technique for embroidering leaves.

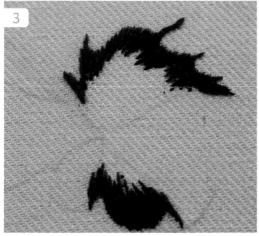

Use thread 998 to embroider the outer layer of leaf 7, and use threads 998 and 588 to embroider half of leaf 8.

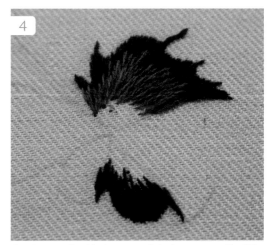

Continue embroidering toward the inner part of leaf 7 using thread 904.

Finally, fill the leaves 7 and 8 completely with thread 477.

🧶 Back Stitch—Detached Continued

This stitching technique bears some resemblance to the raised stem band stitch, with the difference lying in the way the threads are wrapped.

Prepare the threads you will use.

First, start with thread 904 from the base of leaf 5, using the stem stitch to create parallel lines. Then, switch to thread 588 and use a split stitch to embroider from the leaf tip as shown in the picture, down to below the first horizontal line.

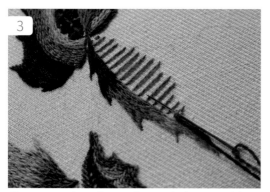

Then, start to loop the needle over the bottom of the first horizontal line and pull tight.

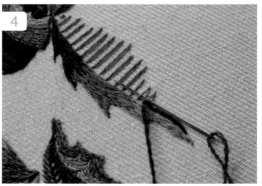

Next, double back, simultaneously looping over the first and second horizontal lines, then pull tight again.

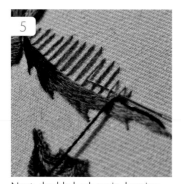

Next, double back again, looping over the second and third horizontal lines, then pull tight. The next step is to loop over the third and fourth horizontal lines, and so on. Note that the needle does not need to penetrate the fabric here.

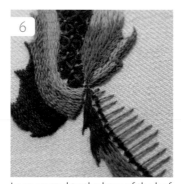

Loop around to the base of the leaf segment as shown in the picture, then take the needle to the back side, and secure the stitches using the three stitch technique.

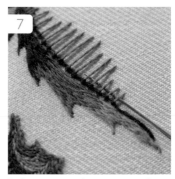

Before starting the next row of wrapping, extend the needle below the horizontal line and tidy up the first row of stitches, ensuring they are as close to the left half of the leaf segment as possible.

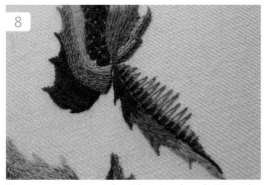

Continue wrapping to the right using threads 904 and 477.

Finish by wrapping with thread 854 to complete the entire leaf segment. The final effect is as shown in the picture. This stitching technique, compared to raised stem band stitch, has a more three-dimensional appearance.

🧶 Laid Work Stitch, Diamond Trellis Stitch

For leaf 9, start by using thread 588 to embroider with laid work stitch as the base, leaving the middle part for the leaf vein.

Then, use threads 904 and 758 to embroider a single layer of diamond trellis stitch (refer to page 27), completing the upper half of the leaf surface with reference to the arrangement of the lower half of the leaf surface as shown in the picture.

On top of the completed diamond trellis stitch, use thread 904 to lay another layer of thread at approximately a 45-degree angle, converging with the intersection points of the first layer from the previous step. Finally, use thread 588 to nail sesame and secure the intersections.

🧶 Palestrina Stitch

This is a technique primarily based on surface stitching. While it can be done with double threads, for instructional purposes, a single thread has been used here.

Next, we will use the new stitching technique Palestrina stitch to embroider the veins of leaf 9. As shown in the picture, use thread 716 to stitch downward from the top, then bring the needle out from the midpoint on the left side of this stitch.

After bringing the needle out, pass it from right to left through the bottom of the stitch made in the previous step.

After tightening, you will see that the lifted thread is divided into two parts. We will temporarily call the lower part "B."

As shown in the picture, the needle passes from the upper right to the lower left, pressing down on the thread and passing through the lower part of B.

After passing through B, pull downward to tighten, forming a knot.

Repeat step 1, taking a small stitch, with the entry point slightly to the right of the drawn line.

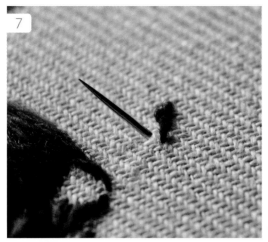

7

Bring the needle out from the middle position on the left side of the stitch.

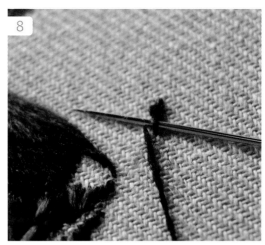

8

Pass the needle to the right and through the bottom of the stitch.

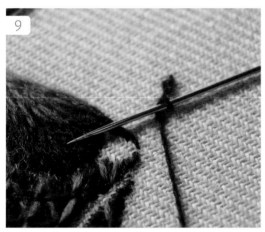

9

As in step 4, pass the needle from upper right to lower left, pressing down on the thread, and pull to tighten, forming a knot.

10

Repeat the above steps to complete a row of Palestrina stitches.

11

Next, snugly above the first row, use thread 758 to complete the second row.

12

The picture shows the detailed effect.

🧶 Whipped Wheel Stitch

This is a technique primarily based on surface wrapping, commonly used for quick filling of large areas.

Next, embroider leaf 10 using a new stitching technique, the whipped wheel stitch. Prepare the embroidery thread you will be using.

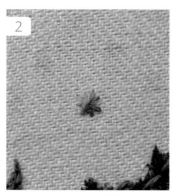

Start by using thread 403 to work straight stitches to form the shape of an asterisk, i.e., first create a cross, then another cross intersecting at a 45-degree angle.

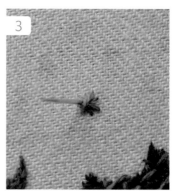

Next, bring the needle out from one of the 45-degree angles on the top left, as close to the center point as possible.

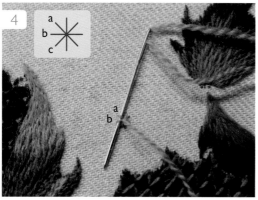

You can switch to a tapestry needle at this point. As shown in the picture, pass it through the bottom of the two threads (a and b), then pull tight.

Now wrap around b and c.

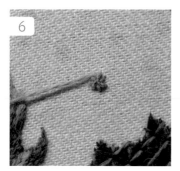

Continue in this manner, wrapping the threads until there is no more space left to wrap around.

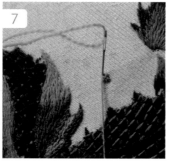

Finally, bring the thread to the back, flip the embroidery hoop over, and use the remaining thread to weave back and forth across the stitches on the back 2 to 3 times for securing. Then, cut the thread.

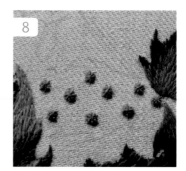

Repeat the above steps, and the effect will resemble a group of small cookies.

⬡ French Knot, Back Stitch, Whipped Wrap Stitch

Use a water soluble pen to make marks on leaf 10 as shown in the picture.

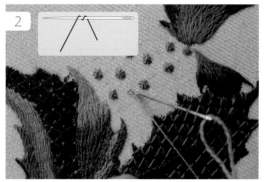

Next, use thread 403 along with the French knot to embroider the marked parts. Here's a brief description of French knot technique: Bring the needle up through the fabric. With thread in the left hand and needle horizontally in the right hand, wrap the thread around the needle 2 to 3 times from top downward (as shown in the diagram). Push the wrapped needle down through the fabric, and pull the thread until a knot forms.

The picture shows the effect of the French knot. Finish all of them at the blue points.

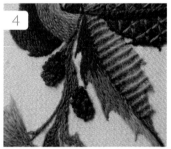

Use the French knot to complete the two mulberries below leaves 1 and 5.

Go back to leaf 10 and use the remaining thread from steps 2 to 3 to outline the outer edge of the leaf with back stitch.

Then, use thread 567 to wrap the thread from the outside to the inside (or from the inside to the outside), ensuring that each stitch passes through every stitch of the back stitch. Pull tight before continuing to wrap around the next stitch. I named this stitch technique whipped wrap stitch, which can be used to thicken any outline, such as the outline formed by the stem stitch and the split stitch.

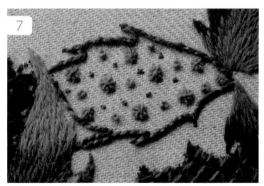

As shown in the picture, use thread 834 to add another layer of whipped wrap stitch, resulting in a solid appearance.

🧵 Diamond Trellis Stitch, Laid Work Stitch

We will embroider leaf 11 using a set of blue purple threads. For ease of embroidery, rotate the image 180 degrees.

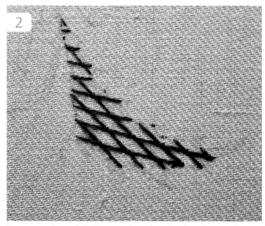

First, use thread 567 to embroider the first layer of grids, then use the same colored thread to secure the intersections of the grids.

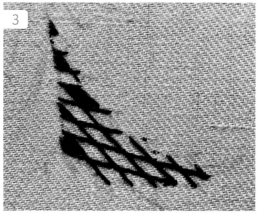

Fill in several empty grids intermittently using thread 567.

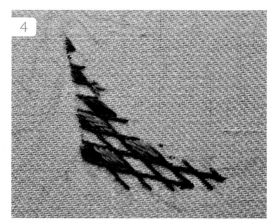

Next, fill in the adjacent three grids using thread 484. The principle here is to avoid having grids of the same color adjacent to each other.

Finally, fill in the remaining grids using threads 894 and 744.

🧶 Burden Stitch

Review the burden stitch (refer to page 55) and embroider leaf 12.

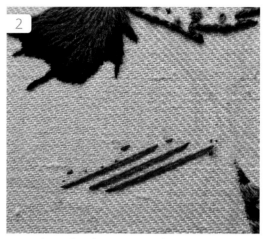

Rotate the embroidery piece 180 degrees. First, use thread 904 to pull three horizontal lines.

Then, use the same colored thread to complete the first layer from top to bottom.

Continue by stitching downward using thread 477.

Finally, finish off with thread 854.

🪡 Bullion Knot Stitch

Use the bullion knot stitch (refer to step 11 on page 90) to complete the other half of leaf 12.

A quick review of the bullion knot stitch: pull out the double thread from point A, enter at point B, then return to point A and exit halfway.

Use your thumb and forefinger to assist in wrapping the thread around the exposed half needle four times.

Then, firmly pinch the loops with both fingers and pull the needle through.

Finally, bring the needle to the back at the position shown in the picture to complete the stitch. Repeat the above steps using different colored threads to complete leaf 12.

Use the same stitching technique to complete the silkworm above leaf 10.

The threads for the silkworms are 744 and 894, alternating between them. The picture shows the details of the silkworm.

Quickly review the fishbone stitch (see page 38) and the back stitch—detached continued (see page 108).

For ease of embroidery, the embroidery piece is turned upside down. The four curved sections in the middle of leaf 13 are all stitched using the fishbone stitch with thread 588, starting from the tip of the leaf and working towards the base. It is important to note that since the outer curved lines are longer than the inner ones, the angle of the outer curve should be larger when turning, allowing for a smooth transition.

Right next to the fishbone stitch is a series of back stitch—detached continued with threads 854, 477 and 904 from left to right.

On the right side of leaf 13 (as shown by the red arrow), we will use threads 403 and 834. First, use thread 403 to create four sets of sparse buttonhole stitches, then use thread 834 to fill in the gaps with straight lines. Finally, embroider two small cookies made up of whipped wheel stitch in the remaining two spaces.

The left half of leaf 13 (as shown by the red arrow) will be completed using a set of four colored threads combined with chain stitch. You can refer to the neck feather section of the mandarin duck in chapter four (see page 84).

As shown in the picture, the threads from the bottom up are 854, 477, 904, and 998, from lightest to darkest.

🪡 Spider Web Stitch

The spider web stitch is similar to the previously learned whipped wheel stitch. Both techniques start with a cross stitch grid and then proceed to wrap thread around it on the fabric, creating a three-dimensional effect.

Prepare the threads and get ready to learn the spider web stitch.

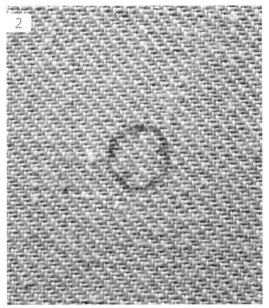

Since the actual spider web in the embroidery pattern is too tiny for effective teaching, it will be demonstrated separately. First, draw a circle using a water soluble pen as shown in the picture, and mark five equally spaced points along the inner circle.

From each of the five small points, stitch towards the center point as shown in the picture.

After completing the stitches, end the thread using the three stitch technique.

Take another color of embroidery thread and bring the needle out at the upper left corner.

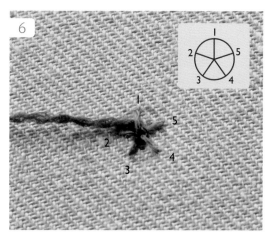

Start wrapping the thread around, moving up and down. As shown in the picture, the blue thread passes below 2, above 3, below 4, above 5, below 1 and so on.

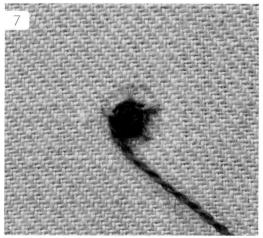

The only thing to pay attention to during wrapping is the tension of the thread. Keep it moderate.

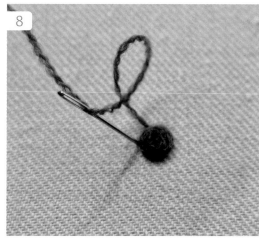

Once the green baseline is fully covered, bring the needle to the back to complete the stitch.

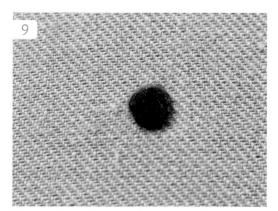

The completed effect is as shown in the picture.

The outer space of leaf 14 is decorated with the spider web stitches. If you want to achieve the fluffy effect required in previous cases, the thread should be relaxed appropriately during the wrapping process and not pulled too tight.

Going back to the previous leaf, we use the thread 904 to apply coral stitch (refer to page 33) to outline leaf 12.

Next, use some small stitches to complete the branches. Use thread 834 for back stitch, then use the same color for wrapping.

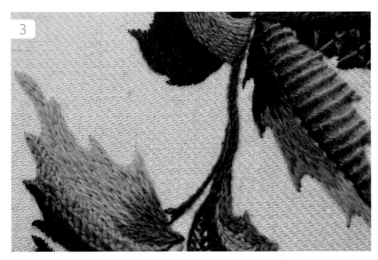

The finished effect is as shown in the picture.

Returning to leaf 14, here we will learn a stitching technique called "couching stitch" for outlining. The special feature of this stitch is that it uses two threads simultaneously for embroidery. The thread being secured can be a single strand or multiple strands. Here we are using a single strand. As shown in the picture, use the green thread 834 to stitch along the outer contour of the leaf, then use the light green thread 403 to couch thread 834 in place for shaping.

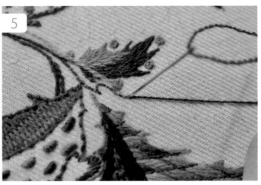

The spacing between the couched threads is generally around 3 mm. When turning corners, bring the green thread to the back, then come out right next to it and continue couching. Complete the outer contour of leaf 14 in this manner.

Butterfly

🧶 Turkey Rug Stitch

This is a very interesting stitching technique, originating from the weaving method of Turkish carpets, particularly suitable for depicting the hair of animals and humans.

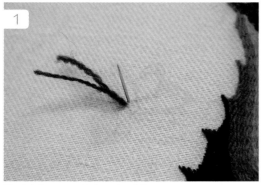

The Turkey rug stitch evolved from carpet weaving. First, using double stranded thread 588, without starting the stitch or knotting the thread end, insert the needle directly at the indicated point, then come out next to it.

The third stitch is inserted between the first and second stitches.

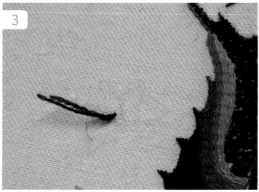

Pull the thread to the back to tighten the stitching, this is the first set of stitches, aiming to secure the thread ends on the embroidered surface.

Next, embroider the second set of stitches. The needle comes out from the middle below the stitch formed in the previous step.

Then, come in next to the right side, leaving a small gap between the exit and entry points, and leaving a loop of thread on the embroidered surface.

Exit toward the right side.

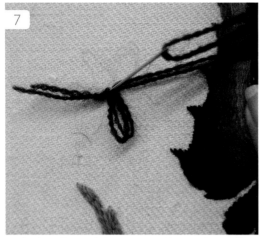

Go back to the gap left in step 5 and insert the needle.

The loop created in step 5 is secured in place.

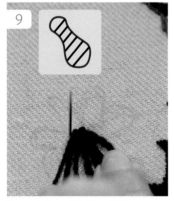

Repeat steps 4 to 8 until the butterfly's body is embroidered in rows (as shown in the diagram).

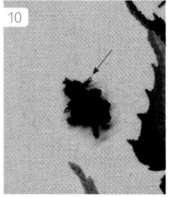

For the final stitch (as indicated by the red arrow), pull it directly onto the embroidered surface, leaving a short length, and then cut it off directly.

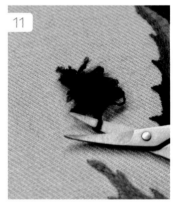

Next, use scissors to cut each loop in half on the embroidered surface.

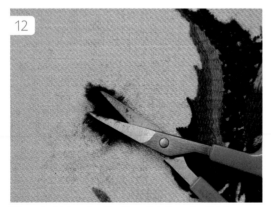

Then start trimming the threads left on the fabric surface. Remember, take it slow and steady, like trimming your hair. Do not rush.

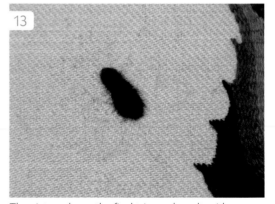

The picture shows the final trimmed result, with the middle higher and the two sides lower. After completion, flip the embroidery frame over and gently pat to remove any loose threads on the embroidered surface. If there are still fine debris, you can use a soft bristled toothbrush to brush it off.

🧶 General Application of Stitching Techniques

Finally, let's complete the butterfly's wings.

First, use thread 489 with long and short stitch to lay the foundation. Leave gaps along the outer edges of the wings.

Then, use dark green thread 835 to outline the wings with the long and short stitch.

Next, use thread 567 to embroider laid work stitch for the butterfly's head. If one layer is not thick enough, embroider another layer directly above it. Then, refer to the pistil stitch used for completing the flower pistils in chapter three (see page 66) and use thread 403 to complete the butterfly's antennae. Finally, with the remaining thread 403, stitch several scattered small sesame seeds on top of the butterfly's wings, and the butterfly is complete.

Before completing the entire piece, observe which areas need fine tuning. For example, in leaf 6, we can work two sets of back stitch—detached continued (refer to page 108) to make the details of the leaf more compact.

The picture shows the improved effect. During the embroidery process, you will realize that stitching techniques can be combined flexibly, creating more possibilities beyond their individual use.

7

Use thread in the same color palette along with stem stitch to outline the edges of some leaves. Leaves that require outlining refers to those whose edges appear somewhat irregular and need outlining to define them.

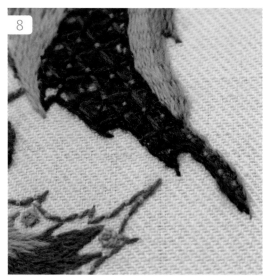

8

The image above shows the result of outlining the edge of leaf 1.

9

Using the same technique, complete outlining for the remaining leaves that require it.

10

Overall, in this embroidery piece, the leaves that require outlining are mostly those embroidered with trellis stitch.

11

This piece is complete.

APPENDICES

Index of Stitches